T0381012

Knowing His Presence
KABOD

THE PHYSICAL WEIGHT OF GOD!

CHIOMA AFOKE

authorHOUSE®

AuthorHouse™
1663 Liberty Drive
Bloomington, IN 47403
www.authorhouse.com
Phone: 833-262-8899

Published by AuthorHouse   10/29/2024

ISBN: 979-8-8230-3201-8 (sc)
ISBN: 979-8-8230-3202-5 (hc)
ISBN: 979-8-8230-3203-2 (e)

Library of Congress Control Number: 2024919383

Print information available on the last page.

This book is printed on acid-free paper.

Contents

Contents

Chapter One

The Physical Presence of God

The physical presence of God is a certain location, point or person where God is in a concentrated form. When you step into an atmosphere like this, you will be able to perceive, and see the physical movements of God. The Israelites encountered this presence as a shadow, the pillar of cloud by day, and a pillar of fire by night. The Israelites walking out of Egypt, experienced him as a pillar of Cloud by day, and at night he was known as a pillar of Fire, (Exodus 13:21).

You know when you enter a certain location in your home, where your flavor otherwise known as your body's natural perfume is in a concentrated form, you can identify it as your habitat. Also, when you get into a certain location, where some animals live, even before you see them physically, you would have experienced their flavor, their natural odor. This is what it feels like to walk into an atmosphere called the presence of God. Your ability to discover this kind of sites or locations, and or persons on the earth is equivalent to finding treasures.

There are certain persons who God has chosen to be carriers of such fragrance of his; these persons or places when you encounter them, you would have encountered God somehow. Many things will begin to happen to you, that will make you know that you have encountered God.

Moses said, "if your presence will not go with us, take us not up" (Exodus 34:10). Moses understood that the presence of God is a currency to anything that needs to be achieved during his own time. This presence as he described it, is the personality of God. One man that understood the importance, and cherished the physical presence of God was Moses. From his burning bush experience, crossing the red sea and fighting to cross over to the land that God Promised them, Moses understood that the whole essence of their victories could only be attributed to the physical presence of God that shadowed them. Moses did everything possible to get God to go with them; and as one of the greatest intercessors that ever lived, Moses was able to move the hands of God to favor his people, Israel.

Only a wise leader who understands the secrets to his victory, will do almost anything possible to secure the source of his victory, and Moses did just that. He understood that the origin and the source of the continuance of all the victories from Egypt, to crossing the red see and eventually to getting into the wilderness was nothing humanly and could only be attributed to that magnificent presence of God.

Moses was so humble, and one of the wisest leader in the history of the Bible, who understood timing properly, and knew God to a sustainable extent. Not only did he know when to approach God, he also knew what to say to God. Moses took a great advantage of this privilege of getting to know God physically.

Have you ever wondered what on earth would make a man experience such intimacy with God, and still lead the people correctly? It was because God was physical with Moses. Though, the Israelites experienced God as a cloud of Glory, fire descending on the Mountain, and smoke filling the temple, which were just the few physical manifestation of the real personality of God, the man Moses had a taste of the physical presence of God.

Whenever you are privileged to meet the presence of God, which could be in form of a person or location, know it for a fact that your time of encounter has come. This time of encounters is a season in one's lifetime that can either transform you as a child of God or can consume you. This time of encounters encroaches into your privacy without your permission, it is what I call "knowing the physical presence of God, the Kabod, his heavy weight". Encountering God is a life changing experience; John the beloved in the book of Revelation was brought to the presence of the Lord, and that gave birth to the book of Revelation, and many other testimonies.

My Encounter with the Man Alph Lukau

As I said earlier, certain people or location that you encounter, could be synonymous to encountering God as a person. This is because they carry the presence of God in a concentrated form. I was visiting Johannesburg South Africa in 2018, as a young woman seeking a solution and answers to some of the problems I had. The intensities of the spiritual attacks, and physical manifestation of the dark world around me led me to this man. I came looking for help, seeking to know what I would do to beat the devil as I watch him do.

Alph Lukau is a man that I witnessed physically challenge witches and wizards, and nothing happened to him. Many avoid talking about the devil, his agents, witches, wizards and satanists because they are afraid of the outcome. The man Alph Lukau is not. Before now, I heard stories about Archbishop Idahosa, how he stopped witches from invading his territory Nigeria, and how he manifested the physical presence of God, to the point that the dark world avoided him.

When I saw the man Alph Lukau, how he beat the devils and challenged witches openly, and nothing happened, I got very interested. I needed a man that could show me how to do the same. I was being physically and spiritually attacked and harassed by the dark world, the world of witches was after me, and wanted me by all means.

When I got into one of his services, the atmosphere around him, the charisma, the glory he brought into the place was phenomenal. After one of those services, I asked God, what is it about this man of God, the power, how can I get to be like him, to stop all the harassment. While meditating on that, God spoke to me physically, in my hotel room in Johannesburg. He said, "Why don't you ask to know me?" The voice I heard has become so familiar today as I write this book. Though I was taken back, I had many questions, God just told me I do not know him? And I had been born again for Seventeen years as at that time. I have been through foundational schools, discipleship programs, and other bible schooling provided by the churches. I had served as a welfare minister where I was responsible for programs and the feeding of the men of God who attended these programs. I had served in children ministry, was a member of the church intercessory group. Served as an usher, head usher, was responsible for the church account, making sure that every money was deposited in the bank at the end of services on Sundays. I had the key to the depository of the church funds. All these, and God said, you do not know me. As these thoughts went through my mind, I gave in to God. Remember, God did not say he does not know me, he just told me I did not know him, that's a big difference. God can know all about you, but you know nothing about God.

At the end of the program called IVP (international visitors program) that season, I began to have encounters, better encounters. Remember the encounters I had before meeting Alph Lukau were almost constant harassments from the dark world. During one of those services, the man

4

Alph Lukau, came around me, laid hands upon me, blew some hot air on my head (that's how I interpreted it then). In the same service, he did it again, and again. The third time he came around me, I asked God, "What did I do wrong?" I said this man has blown on my head three times, "Did I do anything wrong?"

Today, I write to tell the world that God can be known, and can be encountered personally, and through men and places. Alleluia Ministries International has become a place of many encounters, above all, Alph Lukau is a place of encounter. He is one man I know, that will make you dream dreams if you stay around him. The presence of God he carries and manifests is a concentration of God and constitutes heaven on earth.

Jesus said in the book of John 17:2, "As thou hast given him power over all flesh, that he should give eternal life to as many as thou hast given him" It is God that gives one the power to manifest eternal life, and this manifestation is in form of giving it out. In other words, when people encounter you as a person or encounter a place, and they get healed of their diseases, freed from oppression, recover from debts, what they have experienced is eternal life. This is why I say that people who carry the presence of God in a concentrated form can be encountered, just as God can be encountered.

The presence of God, His Kabod, the heavy weight of God, the Shekinah glory, you will have to discover and personalize it to yourself. It is that glory that followed the Israelites, that made their enemies fearful of them, and the unseen hands that knocked down the Jericho walls.

It is that glory that David pursued after, the presence he sorted for, which made God call him the man after his own heart. David understood the secret of dwelling in the presence of the Lord, that's why he begged God not to take him away from his presence, and he begged God not to take the Holy Spirit from him. (Psalm 51:11). He saw what happened to Saul, what a life of torment he lived after the Spirit of the Lord departed from him.

David understood that life is meaningless outside the presence of God, the exploits he did as the Shepard boy, and as the king would not have happened without this physical presence of the Father, and he treasured it very much.

David also understood that there is a great connection between the presence of God and the Holy Spirit; of a truth, the presence of God, is the Holy Spirit; he is the one who manifests the physicality of God as a person. In Genesis 1:3 we were told that the Spirit moved upon the face of the deep, then God said…it is the manifestation of God, the movement of the Holy Spirit that was seen here in Genesis 1:3.

It is a very dangerous thing to have the presence of God or be in the presence of the Lord, and not make the most benefit, or exploit of it. Daniel called it "knowing the Lord and doing exploits" Daniel 11:32. To be able to do an exploit for God in the Kingdom, you will need to be able to be in tune with the presence of God; you will need to be able to discern when the Presence of God comes on you, or when you step into the very presence.

Jacob stumbled into the presence of God, which was manifested in form of a dream, when he woke up, he said, "Surely the LORD is in this place, and I knew it not," Genesis 28:16.

What does this mean? It means that you can walk into an atmosphere of God, a location heavily dominated and occupied by God, and not know it. Because you have not developed your sensitivity to the level of discerning the changes in an atmosphere.

As a natural man, there are senses you were endowed with even when in the womb and after your birth that make you move securely and safely in your environment. Your ability to tune in properly and study these senses gives you an edge over other creation on earth. But as a man or a woman who have been baptized into the presence of God, your spiritual senses become the superiority you have over other creation in attaining God's divine purpose on earth. What I am saying is this, when you are baptized into the presence of God, you attain the ability to know God and your environment better, and when you know your environment better, you can be better prepared to life of heaven on earth. You become an endorsement of heaven on earth, and a carrier of the presence of God.

When you are a carrier of the presence of God, there are certain things you will be associated with, the characters of God will be manifested through you. When you go through places or locations, these places and the things around these locations will experience the presence which you carry, the atmosphere which is heaven on earth will be experienced by people and creatures including natural and unnatural things. As one who possesses the presence of God in a concentrated form, you have certain abilities or attributes of God. I will discuss this in detail in a latter chapter of this book, what happens to you and to a place, when you are a carrier of the presence of God in a deposited form.

It's very possible to detect a sudden switch in the atmosphere around you, this is a gift of the Holy Spirit, and you can ask and receive it. When the presence of God is upon you, there are certain manifestations that you will physically observe. In discussing this physical presence of God, we are going to consider some men who came face to face with God, men who really got a touch of the heavy weight of God in the Bible.

Moses and the Physical Presence of God

The LORD said to Moses "I will do this thing that you have said because you have found grace before me, and because I have known you by name" Exodus 33:17. I have known you by name is a very powerful statement coming from the LORD. Can one ever imagine the God who created the heavens and the earth, who has no beginning and has no end, would speak to a man this way? It's incredible! Each time I read this passage in the Bible, it overwhelms me, to even imagine it. Today, I decided to find the true meaning of that statement "I know thee by name" and I am intrigued to discover what God said to Moses.

The Hebrew word used here for "I know you "is the Hebrew word "YADA", a kind of knowledge that comes from experience and by encounter. When you get to know someone closely because you have encountered them, you have experienced the person, God said to Moses I will do what you have asked me to do because I have experienced you, I have encountered you.

It is very interesting that God said to Moses, I know you "By Name"- the Hebrew word used here for name is "Shem" which means reputation, memory, character. In other words, God was saying to Moses, I have experienced your character, your reputation, your honor, and your authority, and I am willing to do what you have said.

It means, God was watching and paying close attention to Moses all the while he was leading his people, how he treated them, and how he interceded for them. God indeed paid close attention to Moses. God pays attention to the things you do, and how you treat people; he considers these things, sometimes when he makes his judgment. A perfect example was when the Amalekites refused that the Israelites would pass through their borders, God recorded it for them, Exodus 17:8-14.

Follow me to Exodus 33:18, where Moses begged God to show him his glory. The Hebrew word for the word "your glory "is the word "Kabod" which means "a great physical weight "a kind of weight that can be seen physically. Moses wanted the manifestation of God to be in form of physical encounter of his real personality.

Let me explain in detail what happened here. The people of Israel were very problematic, especially with obeying God's directions when he led them physically. Their murmurings, and complaints about God and journey, became a hinderance to them getting into the Promised land. God told Moses his servant to tell the people, he will no longer lead them physically. You have to understand the kind and the form of God who led them, was the form of God who could not withstand iniquity, the form of God that consumes, Exodus 33:1-3. This was the form or the aspect of God, the people needed to deliver them from Egypt, the form of God that judges. That's why Egypt experienced all the plagues, because of the form of God that was available to deliver his people.

The people repented and mourned, seeking God's face. They were all in their tents and didn't come close to the tabernacle (which was a meeting place for the people and God).

When Moses entered the tabernacle to commune with God, the physical presence of God descended and stood at the door of the tabernacle in form of a pillar of cloud. The people saw this physical manifestation of God, his shadow, and they all rose and worshipped him. The Bible recorded that "the LORD spoke to Moses' face to face as a friend "Exodus 33:9-11.

When Moses noticed God physically standing at the door of the tabernacle, He said to God "I beseech thee, show me thy Glory." The Hebrew word "show" here is the word "ra-ah" a word that denotes a seeing by physical eyes, sighting, and observing physically.

What Moses was saying to God here is, I can see your shadow standing in front of me, please I beg you, if I found favor in your sight as you just said, open my eyes to see you physically. That's exactly what he was asking for, he had already been accustomed to different versions of the manifestations of God from the burning bush, through the Red Sea, to the top of the Mountains, when he received the tablets of stones. He was not asking for God to manifest to him in form of signs and wonder, he had already experienced those. Moses the servant of the LORD, was ready to physically see what God looked like.

God agreed to Moses's request, told him he would place him on the rock by him which is also significance of the mount that Elijah stood upon in 1 kings 19:11.

In the book of Exodus 34:4-5, Moses hewed two tablets of stones, and rose very early in the morning to meet up with the appointment as initially agreed.

God told Moses, I will show you my back, not my face, because no man can see my face as God and live. He told him to meet him to come the following morning and stand upon a Rock. This Rock is a significance and a representative of the person of God, Exodus 33:21-23, Exodus 34:1-4. Rising early in the morning, Moses took the stones for the commandments, and appeared as instructed of the LORD. The bible said that the LORD descended in the cloud and stood with Moses. One would ask, did Moses see the person of God physically? The bible said The LORD spoke to Moses, face to face. Meaning, the LORD would physically stare at Moses's face, but Moses was not able to see the LORD, because no man could see his face and live, Exodus 34:5-8. Do you know how many times the Lord God would have walked in on you and watched everything you did physically without you knowing it? Just a side statement!

When Moses got to the top of the Mountain as instructed by God, he was already waiting for him. The LORD stood there for sometimes, he proclaimed the name of the LORD as he had promised Moses in the prior chapter when the appointment was being scheduled. The LORD had told Moses that he will cover him with his hand, then when he passes by, he will take away his hand so that Moses could see his back part, Exodus 33:22-23.

This was exactly what the LORD did here. He descended in the cloud, stood with Moses, then he proclaimed his name, then removed his hand from Moses, and once Moses saw his back part, he bowed his head and worshipped the LORD. This was Moses's encounter and experience. The same experience the LORD wanted to give to Elijah, just to reassure him that he is still the LORD, and that he is still very much with him. But Elijah refused this encounter, he had made up his mind, he said no to ministry.

Another way to know that the LORD talked to Moses' face to face was the appearance of his face when he came down from the Mountain after that encounter. The bible said his face shone with light to the level that the people of Israel were unable to look at him directly in the face. Do you know why? That face had been before the physical face of God Almighty, that face saw the back side of God. Exodus 34:29-30. It is significance to mention that the people could not stand his face, due to this encounter he had with God, Exodus 34:34-35.

Elijah and the Physical Presence of God

Elijah the Tishbite, one of the greatest prophets in the Bible, was seen running for his life after a threat from the Queen called Jezebel. He had just concluded a great victorious crusade against false prophets who ate at the Queen's table, which led to the slaughter of over four hundred of them. Jezebel was a well-known daughter of a King of a neighboring country called Zidon. A country which was known for gross wickedness, and idolatry, because they worshipped Baal and Ashtoreth.

When Jezebel whose father was also known as a priest of Baal came into Israel through marriage to the king Ahab, she introduced them to deep Baal worship. As a result of this, God sent Elijah, who did judgment to the prophets of Baal. He slaughtered over four hundred of them in one day. This became a contention between Elijah the Tishbite, and the Queen Jezebel. Elijah being fearful for his life after he received a life-threatening letter from Jezebel, hid himself in a cave (1 kings 19:9). The LORD found him, and asked him "What are you doing here Elijah?" Elijah at this point was moving against the plan of God for his life. The crusade he just concluded at Mount Carmel was the beginning of his ministry. God had told him when the Angel fed him the cake baked on heavenly coals that the journey was just starting; the display between him and the prophets of Baal was just the beginning of his ministry.

You know, what happened at Mount Carmel between Elijah and the prophets of Baal, was a staging of the demonstration of the Power of God, which usually happens before a revival. In other words, it was the beginning of the revival that was needed to bring Israel back to the LORD. God literally just started manifesting his physical presence before Elijah and the people of Israel. He came to them in form fire, consumed the sacrifices placed on the altar at Mount Carmel. At this point, Elijah had his mind made up, to quit ministry.

In 1 Kings 19:11, the LORD told Elijah to stand on a mountain because he wanted to manifest himself to him. God wanted to show himself to Elijah, he wanted Elijah to see a part of him that Moses saw. Unlike

Moses, Elijah said no. God wanted to give Elijah his manifest presence, to reassure him that, he is God, and he was with him.

How do I know this? First, when the word of the LORD came to Elijah while he was hiding in the cave, he said to him "go and stand upon the Mountain" This mountain was a location that had a concentrated form of God because the LORD passes by it frequently. That particular mountain was known for many encounters, Abraham, and Jacob, encountered God on this same mountain. Moses had many encounters with God on this same mountain. The mountain was the Lord's, and it became a place of encounter and reassurance, a place he demonstrated his physical abilities to his prophets. It also means that when God wants to encourage you especially when you are beaten down with the works of life, he will show up physically; you will see him in a form of an encounter or encounters. He is the same yesterday, today and forever.

When God passed by, he stood by Elijah, but Elijah was no longer interested in ministry. Creation around Elijah manifested in response to the physical presence of GOD. The bible said in 1 Kings 19:11-13, a great and strong wind rented the mountain and broke the rocks in 'pieces, before the LORD... and the LORD was not in the wind. Also, an earthquake came, and passed, then a fire, but the LORD was not in the wind, neither in the earthquake nor in the fire. Do you know why the bible said the LORD was not in any of those works of nature? Because, the LORD was standing right there beside Elijah, but Elijah could not see the physical presence of the LORD. These natural things such as the wind, the earthquake, and the fire were all responding to the physical presence of the LORD before Elijah, but Elijah could not perceive the LORD, because he had already withdrawn himself from the LORD.

When the LORD in a still small voice spoke to Elijah, once he perceived the voice of the LORD because at least he was accustomed to hearing the voice of GOD, what Elijah did was shocking. He took his mantle, wrapped his face around and walked away from there. This action was significant, he was basically saying he was done. Not only was he no longer interested in hearing from God concerning ministry, but he also wasn't ready to see any part of God that could make him change his mind about quitting. When he did this, God understood what he was saying, he wasn't going to be convinced by any of the manifestations of the physical presence of God, even his great physical weight.

This is the reason God does not force himself on anyone, not on his servants; he is a gentle Savior. Elijah communicated well enough to God, he was done with ministry, his attitude towards the physical manifestation of God demonstrated it, and that's why God told him to go find Elisha to carry on from him, 1Kings 19:15.

It is very important to reiterate that Elijah quit ministry because of a threat from a witch called Jezebel. This is also the fact today in ministry, many ministers have gone home to be with the Lord, therefore taking an early retirement from ministry due to witchcraft attacks, and oppressions. Witches are known as the core resistance of the prophetic. Whenever you see a prophet who is thriving in ministry, know for a fact, they have either conquered the witches of their households, or in that process. This is the first assignment the Lord will give to you as a prophet, dealing and conquering witches. They are the major problems of prophets.

In conclusion, Elijah did not deal with the witchcraft of his father's house called Jezebel, he returned back as John the Baptist, was beheaded by the same witch (Herodias) who threatened to have his head. (Mark 6:14-29)

David and the Physical Presence of God

David was a man who understood what a true presence of God is worth; to David without the presence of God, his existence was questionable. All the Psalms he wrote was because of the tangible relationship he had with God. David pursued after God early in life, as a Shepard boy he did wonders in the wilderness because the presence of God was physical with him. He was a boy that was taught by God.

David understood that life outside the presence of God was meaningless, and that he could not have achieved all the victories outside the presence of God. He knew how to make God physically present in an environment, a dept which no other prophet attained in the Old Testament.

David's success from killing Goliath to ruling over Israel were all attributed to the physical presence of God that was with him. For this reason, he begged God not to withdraw his presence from him, Psalm 51:11. David also understood that the physical manifestation of the Lord on earth is the person of the Holy Spirit; he is the physical manifestation of God the Father and of Jesus Christ.

David understood the depth of his relationship with God was attributed to physicality of the presence of God. When David said, "What is man that you are mindful of him, and son of man that you visit him?" (Psalm 8:4). He was not only speaking about Adam in the garden, but he was also referring to the physical presence of God around him.

David, being a man who studied and understood the presence of God, provided a blueprint to dwelling in the presence of God. We will look at David's prescription to finding and dwelling in the physical presence of God.

There are details to abiding in God's presence, the word abiding as written in the book of Psalm 15:1, is the Hebrew word guwr (goor) which means to lodge, sojourn, hang out.

According to the Psalm of David Chapter 15; If you must sojourn in the tabernacle of the Lord, his holy place either to worship or lodge, you must learn certain rules. God is not a God of disorderliness, and when you approach his abode, you must present yourself as to his own standards.

Check well, you will see that the word Tabernacle is also the word camp or tent in Hebrew. It is a temporally position which you must attain first before any further physical relationship with God. When you find yourself in the tent of God, you are seen as a sojourner, a visitor; God watches you to see your next step. Some visit and never return back. That is why God takes his time to develop a deeper relationship with man because of man's inconsistence.

What am I trying to say here? I am saying that before there is a dwelling in the presence of the Lord, there is first, a temporal position which you acquire, which is a position of a sojourner, a camper. You know in camping, you don't live there, you only lodge there for some time, then return to your place. I am also saying, you can't dwell in the presence of God without first becoming a sojourner, you visit quiet often, then it will someday become a dwelling place for you.

David started Psalm 15 with a very important question, "Who shall dwell in thy holy hill?" The Hebrew word for dwell as used here in Psalm 15:1, "is the word "Shakan" the word to inhabit, permanent settlement, a permanent stay in the hill or the mountain of the Lord. As believers of Jesus Christ, Mount Zion is where we are currently located, it is our permanent stay and our dwelling place.

Apostle Paul said "You have come unto Mount Zion, the city of the living God, the heavenly Jerusalem… (Hebrew 12:22). There is a city where God dwells, there is where you will locate his street address and number. And if you must visit this city, God is saying don't be deceived, you don't just walk in to collect anything, you don't just see yourself in his presence and make it your personal home, there are guidelines to having a permanent presence of God in your life.

You know, if God truly loves you and wants something deep with you, he will teach you his precepts and the guidelines to his personal presence. Having said that, let me take you through these guidelines for some of you who desire encounters with God, and those who have decided that the encounters are not enough anymore, you now wish to live permanently in the Holy hill of the Lord.

This is my testimony, and I am going to share it with you, God is the same God of the Old and the New, he has not stopped being God, and it is unfortunate that many have been deceived and are now far away from his presence than what he anticipated.

Grace was given to assist you into that permanent dwelling place with the Lord Almighty, it is by his grace that you are drawn closer to his presence, the veil which used to be a separation between you and him has been torn.

If you look at Psalm 15:2, it is the beginning of the answer to that question that was asked in Psalm 15:1. "Lord, who shall abide in thy tabernacle, who shall dwell in thy holy hill?"

"He that walketh uprightly, and worketh righteousness, and speaketh the truth in his heart."

King David is saying here, as a revelation to him and in depth of his personal experience with God, the one who can dwell in God's holy hill, is the one who is able to walk uprightly, one without blemish, whose image is not tarnished, one who is morally justified, without spots and blemish. It is one who can stand and not have Satan standing at his right hand.

This is that woman who maintains her virtue and honors her body as tabernacle of the living God. This person must walk up and right without dodging people because he is ashamed of the atrocities he has committed. It is this person that works righteousness with his fingers and can judge well in the court of the Lord. It is also this person whose heart has no form of deceit, he would not say one thing to the people of God, while his heart is saying something else. This person has no lies in his heart, because your heart speaks first before your mouth. This is the first requirement to having a permanent stay in the presence of God.

15:3 "He that backbiteth not with his tongue, nor doeth evil to his neighbor, nor taketh up a reproach against his neighbor". The person who must enjoy a permanent stay in the holy mount of the Lord, is the person who is not a tale bearer, one who has control over his tongue, and does not use his tongue to destroy others, who will not damage the reputation of his neighbor.

15:4 "In whose eyes a vile person is contemned; but he honoureth them that fear the LORD. He that sweareth to his own hurt, and changeth not." As one who must have a place in the presence of God, not only will you be responsible enough to stand uprightly, but you must also be selective of those who stay around you and are also responsible for those you allow around you. What does that mean you may say? It means exactly what it says, those you allow around you or hang around, must also meet the standard of the level of discipline that you exhibit. In other words, if you don't sleep around or commit impure activities, you cannot have friends or acquittances who are impure at heart (Vile).

Not only would you not associate yourself with such people, but you must also be able to honor those who fear the Lord. In other words, reject those who are known as immoral, then replace them with those who fear the Lord; those who fear the Lord, will likewise live the kind of life that you would find yourself living. This lifestyle is to the point that you would be able to tell the truth regardless of what the consequences would be, even if you must die for the truth, say the truth anyways.

15:5 "He that putteth not out his money to usury, nor taketh reward against the innocent. He that doeth these things shall never be moved". On a final note, according to the Psalm of David, if you must have a permanent location in the presence of God, in the Holy Mount of the Lord, the heavenly Jerusalem, the city of God as rightfully prescribed by Hebrew 12:22, you must not lend your money to people with outrageous interest. Meaning, you lend your money to someone, and they pay you back double of what you loaned them. This person must also not be associated with bribery, especially against an innocent person.

David concluded by saying that this person will never be moved, in other words, no principality, no power, no dominion anywhere will be able to move you out of the place of your stay in the Holy Mount of the Lord.

Chapter Two

The Shadow of God and
The Cloud of Glory

The shadow of God is that cloud of Glory that you would sensationally see before his physical manifestation. When God appears in a place or attends your meetings, you would see this sensational cloud hovering in the atmosphere before his presence is manifested. That cloud of Glory that can be physically seen is the shadow of God.

You see, the Bible often says that the cloud descended before the manifestation; this cloud that descends is the actual shadow of God. For instance, everyone who is a physical person has a shadow that follows them. This shadow is often before or behind the actual person, depending on the sun's position or the light source. If they are directly facing the sun, their shadow is behind them, but if they are backing the sun, their shadow is before them.

When God appears in a place, people most often see his shadow, which is what that Cloud of Glory represents. This cloud that people see descend is a sign that God is around or attending a meeting. Though they may not see God's physical presence, the cloud they see is a sign or a shadow telling them that he is present.

When God walks into a gathering, there is a way to know by observing the kind of cloud you see in the atmosphere, then the manifestation of his physical presence, which outcome is usually healing, deliverance, brokenness, angelic beings, etc., what exactly am I trying to say? When God attends a gathering, a crusade, or any meeting, the resultant effect is usually healings, broken chains, the bonds set free, the hungry receive victory, and many other things that will lead to testimonies.

Let me say it this way: when God physically appears, creation responds to his physical presence. They know how to react to the presence of God better than man. First and foremost, demons run looking out for a hiding place; for example, Jesus finished a forty-day and forty-night fasting in the wilderness, and afterward, he was tempted by the devil. The Bible said he returned in the power of the Spirit, and his fame was announced all over the region of Galilee and the other neighboring towns. Have you asked why his fame was announced? And who made the announcements? Luke 4:14. The demons started responding to the physical presence of God (Jesus), and how they responded to this presence was crying out for help. Jesus entered the synagogue, and the first person who noticed his presence was a demon possessing a man in the temple. The Bible said he cried out, saying, "Let us alone! What have we to do with you, Jesus of Nazareth? Did you come to destroy us? I know who you are—the Holy One of God!" (Luke 4:34).

That's how demons respond to the physical presence of God. The demons know what their destruction looks like and what the actual presence of God is like. When you see a man of God who enters a place, and there is a sudden rumble in that environment, know that there is a physical manifestation of the presence of God through that man of God. Meaning that man that appeared has a level of physical presence of God in them. I will discuss in detail how people can appear and how you see God appear through them.

What I am trying to say is this: the environment or atmosphere and creations, such as plants, rocks, the Wind, etc., have a way of manifesting the presence of God. Whenever the physical presence of God is present, every demonic activity and the environment is captivated and subdued by his presence.

It is like when the president of the USA enters a place, and suddenly, that airspace and the environment become a no-fly zone. In other words, any plane or jet that suddenly tries to fly into that space risks being shut down. Whether it was by mistake or not, they don't take the risk of saying it was a mistake.

Imagine a president taking over airspace; how much more the God who created the airspace? Creation knows who the creator is and how to behave towards God.

If you look at 1 Kings 19:11, when the LORD passed by Elijah the Tishbite, the Wind responded to God's presence by renting the mountain and shattering the rocks in pieces. Afterward, there was an earthquake and then a fire. These were creations' responses to God's physical presence.

Moses was in the wilderness, shepherding the flocks of his father-in-law Jethro, when he suddenly saw a bush burning, but the bush was not consumed. When he turned to see this incredible sight, the LORD spoke to him. In other words, the burning bush and the fire represented the Physical presence of God in that location.

When God appears physically in a location, the atmosphere, the cloud of Glory, creations, and the earth where you stand have a way of telling you that God is around. Even if you are hard of hearing or blind to God's physical presence, which can sometimes happen because of sin or demonic manipulations, you will still be able to sense God's physical presence by the behavior of animate and inanimate objects around you.

Chapter Three

Hosting The Presence of God

Knowing how to host God's presence will make you a sign and a wonder on earth. To consistently host God's presence, you must be obedient to God's word and then obedient to what you hear him say afterward. In Luke 18:1, Jesus advised his disciples that men should always pray and not faint. God will reveal himself to you as you focus on that scripture and meditate on it.

To attract God's presence, consider living a life of prayer. As one thinks in his heart, so is he (Proverbs 23:7). As you consider and meditate on prayer and learn how to live a life of prayer, you will attract God's attention. A practical prayer life is a Godly kind of life because prayer draws you closer to God. Whenever you begin to consider a life of prayer, you are ready to host God's presence; it is God who influences your heart to seek him. David said in Psalm 27:8 "When You said, "Seek My face," My heart said to You, "Your face, LORD, I will seek."

As you begin the journey of a life of prayer, you will begin to grow in the clarity of God's voice.

Let me share with you what happens to me sometimes; when I make up my mind to pray, as soon as I present before God, I wait and pay attention because I expect to hear from God. That's just how I relate to God in the place of prayer. I present my petition, and as I plead, I gain peace, believing he has heard me. Sometimes, even before I conclude my prayer, I get an answer from God. Based on the answer, which sometimes can be in the form of instructions, I am prepared to host him again.

When I pray and fast, it is most times by instructions from God; and as soon as I obey, I come before him, and he opens his arms to me, and the relationship continues. There are many other times when God enters my room without prior instructions; these are the most gracious moments of my life. These are moments when his manifest presence is felt in my room; I feel overwhelmed by this kind of love. I don't take these moments for granted; they are mostly the most powerful moments I have experienced. I literally feel the presence of God in front of me, like he is right in front of me. I hear his voice, and I feel him so close, the fire penetrates my heart and lungs; it is a very euphoric feeling that I do not know how to explain.

In essence, I am saying that God can invite you into his presence, which becomes an encounter for you, but you can also invite God into your arena or your environment by prayer, deep worship, or other spiritual activities. A life of prayer makes God notice your availability. It is left to God to honor your invitation by manifesting his presence.

In addition, for God to come to you physically, you can prepare for his visits, learn to host his presence by acknowledging him, and he will take you further. Be obedient to the word of God, open the word (Bible), and practice living the Bible. Focus on Jesus, try to make the word of God come alive in you, and then you will have God's attention.

To host the presence of God, you must begin by preparing for his visitations; I cannot emphasize this enough: you have to prepare to host God like you host kings. He knows when you want him around, and he will come. Whenever you pray, make room for him, for a conversation with him. Create moments where you will sit there and tell him he is welcome to talk to you, to come to you, and to sit with you. The Holy Spirit is a person who has feelings, and if you appreciate and hunger for his visitations, he will come, and he will teach you how you can always make him come around. Make out time, create dates and times where all you will do is turn off your phones and every distraction and focus on him.

I know you may question my sayings based on theology: God is in you; how do you prepare to host another form of God? Let me ask you, why would God tell Moses to come to the mountaintop at a specific time? (Exodus 34:1-2). Why would God ask Elijah to meet him by the Clift of the Rock? (1 Kings 19:11) If you think these were Old Testament events, why would Jesus leave a particular place and time to another location to be with his Father (God)? Why would he send the crowd away and then go somewhere to pray?

Jesus practiced a life of prayer, a life of hosting the presence of the Father. That's why he always referred people to the relationship he had with his Father, (John 8:28-29). In one of those meetings, he encountered Moses and Elijah; thus, the mount was called the Mount of Transfiguration (Matthew 17:1-3).

Hosting the physical presence or the manifest presence of God is not for religious minds; you would not understand this form of manifestation of God; it is a life of the supernatural.

Let me tell you the truth: most times, when I have appointments with the Holy Spirit, such as the days that I write, he is usually very physical with me. He gives me breaks to eat, care for my kids, and other things, which he usually tells me when to return. And 100% of the time, by the time I get back to the place where I write, he is already there waiting for me.

Sometimes, I get there later than I was told, but as I grew in my relationship with the Holy Spirit, I realized how sensitive he is and how foolish my behaviors were, like taking my time to do things that were time-sensitive to him. I took his presence for granted; it's a special grace that sometimes I feel abnormal if he withdraws from me.

Child of God, you can have the presence of God manifested physically to you, follow you around, and have a conversation with you like Abraham in Genesis 18:17-33.

All you need to do is desire for it, pray continually, and make it a habit. And live a life controlled by the Holy Spirit; he will manifest more to you.

Another way to host the presence of God is through worship: as a child of God, you don't know what true worship does to God. A prophet of God said the only thing God cannot do is to worship himself. That's why He seeks worshippers; yes, you heard me right. If you know how to worship God very well, God will seek after you, meaning God will look for you. Jesus said in the book of John 4:23 " But the hour is coming, and now is, when the true worshipers will worship the Father in spirit and truth; for the Father is seeking such to worship Him." The word seeks here is the Greek word "zetei," Which is an action word that means to search out the root of a matter. It is also the same word as "investigate, inquire, etc. Jesus was indeed saying that the Father searches and inquires for true worshippers.

What qualifies one as a true worshiper here, as described by Jesus, is one's ability to focus on God spiritually and truthfully during worship. It is tough to find true worshipers because many who do it either do it fleshly or to entertain.

Whenever you find a true worshiper, you have seen God's friend; this person does not remain the same. And if you can learn to give God true worship, he will always seek your presence because he knows he will get true worship whenever you are around.

The most crucial way of hosting God's presence is getting accustomed to his word. Most times, when God speaks, he speaks through his word. You may just be reading the Bible, and the word of God will come alive to you. God knows when and to whom to show himself; by this, I mean God can choose you to be someone he wants to manifest his presence to. Whenever this happens, you must continue hosting his presence by getting acquainted with his word (the Bible).

The book of Samuel is an example of this; Eli and Samuel were in the same house, though the word of the LORD was scarce in those days, and there weren't many visions, but God found a way to speak to Samuel. Do you know why the voice of God was so scarce and why God wasn't showing himself or appearing to people? Because he had nobody to speak to and no one seemed to be available, 1 Samuel 3:1. What do I mean by this? I am saying that no one was available to hear from God, and God knows when a man is ready to hear from him. No one was available or dedicated enough to hear from God.

Eli was there, but the voice of the LORD was still scarce because God chooses who and when to speak and appear to people. Eli, by character, did not make himself available to hear the voice of the LORD, but once Samuel became available in the temple, God showed up and started speaking to him. As a result of Samuel's availability, something uncommon became very common. The LORD appeared to Samuel and came to him every time he was at Shiloh. The Bible said that God revealed himself to Samuel through his word. 1 Samuel 3:21. Shiloh here represents a place of deep worship, where all your attention is yielded to God. Child of God, he will show up once you make yourself available and consecrate yourself before him.

Another way to host the presence of the LORD is by living a consecrated life. As we read in the above scripture, 1 Samuel 3, Samuel was consecrated to God by his mother Hanna, who presented him as a servant to the Lord. You know something, child of God: the Lord needs people who will dedicate their lives to his service; once you dedicate your life to his service and live a consecrated life, God will be around you. He is a Holy God; if you want him around, live a consecrated and holy life, and you will have his attention. Have you noticed in the scripture how God bragged about those who lived perfectly for him? Job 1:6: God pays attention to the way you live your life.

Samuel was also said to be perfect before God, and none of his words fell to the ground; meaning everything Samuel spoke about came to pass because he lived a consecrated life. Choose a holy life and make yourself available, and you will begin to host his presence when you catch his attention.

Finally, in hosting the presence of God, you must get rid of the witchcraft-infested environment you find yourself. Yes, I know you would say, isn't the presence of God what drives evil from an environment? But I tell you, witchcraft is the work of the flesh, and what a witchcraft-infested climate does is try to prevent access to the Glory of God; a witch will make sure you don't experience or have access to the glory of God, which goes with his presence. The Spirit of God is very sensitive to your environment, and there are specific environments in which he would not physically visit you. Not because anyone restricts his movements but because he would not interact with you there.

One thing I realize when hosting the presence of God is that I must determine the atmosphere in which I find myself. I can change the vibes and any corrupted atmosphere to an atmosphere conducive to the Holy Spirit by aligning with the Spirit of God in me. For this to happen, your spirit must be in tune with the Spirit of God. In other words, you must learn how to align with the Holy Spirit to host the presence of God. As much as you can change the atmosphere because of the presence of the Holy Spirit in you, it will do you good to live in an atmosphere where the presence of God can easily flow.

God wanted to manifest to Elijah in a tangible form; he told him to go to the Rock before the Lord 1 Kings 19:11, and to Moses, he said to come up to the mountain. (Ex 24:12). Yes, God has preferences when it comes to environmental visitations. There are certain environments which carry God's presence in more concentrated forms than others, and you must prepare your environment for God to visit you. To preserve your environment for God's visitation, you must be very sensitive to the activities you allow; the music you listen to, and the conversations you hold.

Chapter Four

The Physical Manifestation of God's Presence

Proof that God is Physically Present

Certain angels only operate when God is present; the presence of these angels is a confirmation that God is physically present. Gabriel told Zachariah, "I am Gabriel that stands in the Presence of God..." Luke 1:19. Gabriel is saying that certain angels are allowed access in the presence of God, and he is one of them. The presence of God is a very significant place you could ever find yourself. The physical presence of God means one thing: you have a heavenly visitation, and you are in for an encounter.

When Gabriel said, "I am ...and I stand in the presence of God," it meant a lot to him because where God goes, Gabriel also goes. Gabriel is one of those graced angels who accompany God. Gabriel is the messenger of the Lord, so he is like a waiter to God. Because of the nature of his assignment, Gabriel occupies a critical position before God. He only appears with a message when the message is very significant to God. Gabriel shows up whenever a message concerns the future or the next generation.

Gabriel holds a significant position and doesn't take it lightly. That's why he was offended when Zachariah questioned his authority. To him, just showing up to Zachariah alone was significant enough for him to believe him. Zachariah was ignorant of an angelic visitation at that point, though he was a priest, angelic visitations were not that common in Israel. Zechariah was just a religious priest faithful in his religious rituals.

Gabriel knew what it meant to stand in God's presence; he understood God's abilities. It's a very critical position; you cannot entertain doubts. God cannot stand iniquity, whoever would stand before him must stand in complete righteousness.

Lucifer was another angel who manifested the physical presence of God before his fall. He was a messenger angel specially anointed to offer guidance as a Cherub in the Garden of Eden. Though Lucifer was stationed in Eden, he walked on hot stones of fire in the Mount of the LORD (Ezekiel 28:14). Lucifer had two assignments: first as a cherub and second as a light bearer, an illuminator, one who possessed knowledge and a dispenser of information. As a Cherub, he stood before God in worship, and as a protector and keeper of God's interest on earth, he had a responsibility to govern the stars of God. He moved up and down before God and had a stationary place in the Garden called Eden.

Let me tell you how Lucifer got to Eden. Lucifer, son of the Morning (Isaiah 14:12), was one of those angels before the throne, as mentioned in Ezekiel 1:5 and Revelation 4:6. At a point when God created man before Adam, Lucifer was taken from among the four living creatures before the throne, and was specially anointed to cover Eden, with the abilities to walk up and down the mount of the Lord, a unique ability, which was withheld from Adam. Let me explain further: when God anointed Lucifer, he allowed him the ability to maintain his position as an angel who walked on the coals of fire, an ability which he still maintained until he was cast out of heaven. Even though his assignment after he was anointed was to cover Eden and the earth, he could still appear before the Mount of God and walk on coals of fire. God didn't need to visit him the way he visited Adam in the Garden. Adam had a different relationship with God; his assignment was to guard the Garden from the fallen creatures, which included the old serpent, and to rule as the replica of God on earth.

God visited Adam regularly; that was his relationship with him. When Adam fell, God sent them out of the Garden and immediately positioned another set of angels called Cherubim and the double flaming sword at the exact location where Adam was taken, the same position Lucifer fell from.

"So, God drove the man out; and at the east of the Garden of Eden He [permanently] stationed the cherubim and the sword with the flashing blade which turned round and round [in every direction] to protect and guard the way (entrance, access) to the tree of life, (Genesis 3:24).

In other words, when Lucifer fell, Adam was created to replace him in the Garden, and God visited him regularly. During one of those visits, God noticed that man was lonely and gave him a mate. God tried to protect man from the sin of Lucifer, who wanted to become like God. He realized the sin of Lucifer and then created man to be like him (God), but man still fell.

God didn't see the need for a Cherub to continue to guard the Garden of Eden after Adam was created. Therefore, he gave the Job to Adam. "Then the LORD God took the man and put him in the Garden of Eden to tend and keep it. (Genesis 2:15).

Let me explain a little further. Eden was a resting place for God, like an ark, where he retired to rest. That is why God walked through Eden in the cool of the day when he visited Adam.

God didn't create Eden for Adam; he planted a garden in Eden for himself. He imported the Garden from somewhere; it was fashioned for rest whenever God visited the man on the earth, a place of communion between God and the man he had created.

Many of us have houses, and in our houses, we carve out a garden where we would hang out in the evenings to rest and chat with our loved ones. That was exactly what the Garden of Eden represented to God. He created the earth for man, planted a Garden inside the same world he created for man, and then asked the man to dress the Garden for him. In the cool of the day, God will leave heaven (his official place) and come down to the earth in the Garden to chat with a man he created in his image.

The position where Gabriel stands is a position that other angels have held in the past, but they lost their positions due to sin. Do you remember that the Bible mentions in Jude 1:6 certain angels who did not stay within their domain and lost their positions? Because of that, they are also in eternal chains.

Do you know why? By the Holy Ghost, I understand that these angels stood before God, so they have deeper secrets of God. They know a little more than Lucifer, and it would be dangerous to allow them freedom. They would destroy humanity even with the little that they were opportune to see from standing in the presence of God.

God's presence is a significant honor one could have in life. The ability for God to seek you or attend your gathering is overwhelming; it's the highest honor you can get as a man. Many are seeking after God in their different ways, but for God to pursue you or be part of what you are doing is a great honor. That's what Adam had at the Garden; he lost it to sin. God would come down to the earth he created to visit the man he made in his image on the earth; there is nothing more significant than that.

Moreover, the Presence of the Lord is quite adorning. It's a place of encounters; Moses encountered God in the burning Bush, Elijah by the Clift of the rock, and Isaiah when King Uzziah died in Isaiah chapter six. Peter, James, and John encountered God at the Mount of Transfiguration, leaving a significant stain of Glory on them. The presence of God is a place of encounters, which are usually life-changing experiences.

John the Beloved had an encounter that gave birth to the Book of Revelation and many other testimonies. Because of what he was carrying inside of him, John's life was preserved until he reached the Isle of Patmos. The encounter John had was given to him on the Morning of resurrection, which he called "The Lord's Day." Jesus, who died on the cross, and John, being privileged to have witnessed the last moments, went home with Mary, the mother of Jesus, as was instructed by Jesus at the cross. John 19:26-27.

John began his encounters during Jesus' death and resurrection, which gave birth to the book of Revelation. This information is contentious, and I understand, but I will unpack it slowly so you can understand it. In the book of Revelation 10:8-11, John received an instruction to take a book from an angel and to eat the book. Afterward, he was told he would prophesy again to people, nations, tongues, and kings.

The information John released in the Book of Revelation was partly given to him as loaded data, but in the process, Herod tried to kill him to prevent the book from being written. Though Herod was not acting independently, he was under the enemy's influence, trying to avert the book from being released. John's life was preserved because of the data downloaded into him on the Morning of Jesus' resurrection. That's why they couldn't kill him even though they tried multiple times.

Jesus mentioned his plan for John when Peter was offended at John involving himself in his moment with Jesus. John often referred himself to the Disciple whom Jesus loved. John 13:23, John 21:20

It is hazardous to have God's presence or to be in God's presence and not reap the full benefits. Daniel called it knowing the Lord and doing exploits (Daniel 11:32). To exploit God in the Kingdom, you must always be in tune and in season. You must discern when the Presence of God comes on you and when you step into it.

Jacob stumbled into the presence of God; his encounter was in the form of a dream, and when he woke up, he said, "Surely the LORD is in this place, and I knew it not." Genesis 28:16.

What does this mean? It means that you can walk into an atmosphere of God and not know it because you lack spiritual sensitivity and cannot discern changes in an atmosphere. It's possible to detect a sudden change in the atmosphere around you. It is a gift of the Holy Spirit that you can ask for and receive; Apostle Paul called it the discerning of spirits (1 Corinthians 12:10). You can indeed walk into an environment and discern the presence of strange spirits or demons. Even the natural person without a developed spiritual mind can detect a strange presence, which people call goosebumps. It's a way your natural skin reacts to an environment.

As mentioned at the beginning of this Chapter, there are certain angels; when you see them, you know that God is physically present. Lucifer, who is also known as Satan and Devil, was an angel that was accustomed to the presence of God; that's the reason he hates it so much when you try to enter the presence of God because he knows that presence could change your life as a believer of Jesus Christ. When you enter your father's presence (ABBA Father), you can negotiate your matter and intercede for others.

Satan will fight you with everything in him to make sure you do not approach the throne of God or have access to that throne. He understood something about the presence of God, that it changes anything; he knew that because he was an angel of that presence (Ezekiel 28:14). He walked up and down the Mount of God until sin was found in him.

One of his Job as an archangel before God was to lay reports of whatever was happening in the territory he was given to govern (the earth, Eden, the Garden of God). Because it was his Job to govern the earth and keep Eden, the Garden of God, he had access to a level of information and was privy to a certain knowledge of God. Lucifer couldn't have rebelled against God if he didn't master the presence of God to a level; he thought he knew God. Be careful when you think or believe you know God; you cannot know God completely.

There is a level of God he will not reveal to man because he knows man's frame. The Glory of God is hidden in his secrecy (Proverbs 25:2). Whenever you can get the revelation of the secrets of the Lord, then you have discovered secrets to a glorious life. God enjoys being sought after; he is the creator, and in everything he created, he left a space for himself, a representative of his DNA in every one of his creation which is like his signatory.

Lucifer was cast out of heaven by another arc angel called Michael (Jesus testified about this in Luke 10:18, that he was a witness to what happened to Satan in heaven), and he was denied access into the presence of God.

When Adam was created and given charge to govern the same earth and the Garden, Lucifer was jealous and worked so hard until he took that access back from Adam in Genesis Chapter Three.

When he gained access to God's presence, he walked back and forth between the earth and heaven to appear before God. During a general assembly where all the angels gathered to meet with God, Satan would show up. On one of those occasions, God asked him where he was coming from.

Let me explain further, when God asked him in the book of Job 1:7, "Where have you come from?", meaning where is your base now? The word "Where or whence" as used there is a Hebrew word "Ayin" which denotes fatherless, a non-entity, or non-existence. He was used to the presence of God; he needed any means to appear before God. On a good day, what God demanded from Lucifer was a report of what was happening on the earth, but since he became a sinful one, God no longer required his opinion because another had taken his position.

What I am trying to say here is that the report Satan appeared to give to God during the gathering was part of his job description as Lucifer, but he lost it to sin. When Satan appeared before God, rather than give God pleasant information about the earth, he began to accuse Job. Satan had no position with a delegated assignment and no reason to appear before God. Still, since Adam relinquished his authority to him and had nothing to discuss, God decided to discuss Job with him. God was proud of Job and bragged about him before Satan. That's what a great father does over his children; he is proud of them.

Cherubim are known to be angels of God's presence; they stand around the throne of God, and anytime God moves physically, he moves with them, meaning they are part of his entourage.

Genesis 3:8 &10 states, "And they heard the voice of the Lord God walking in the Garden in the cool of the day…And he said, I heard thy voice in the Garden, and I was afraid, because I was naked; and I hid myself."

When Adam said to God, "I heard your voice in the garden." who do you think God was talking to or talking with? Let me explain what happened here, as I was privileged to know by the Holy Ghost. This Garden at Eden, as I said earlier, was a meeting point and a place of communion for God and man (Adam).

God is relational, he didn't create man and left him alone to himself, he visited him regularly. That is why David said in Psalm 8:4 "What is man that you are mindful of him, and the son of man that you visit him?" Because God would walk down in Eden to visit Adam and find out how he was doing. That's how he found out that Adam was lonely and gave him the woman.

Eden was like a replica of the Tabernacle that he gave to Moses; it was a resting place for God on earth. And as it happened the day that man sinned, God was coming for his routine visit and conversing with his entourage, the angels of his presence. While God was talking with his entourage, he noticed that Adam was not in his position; he called out in worry, "…Adam, where are you?" Genesis 3:9. The Hebrew word "where are you," as used there is the word "ay," the same word as "how and what"? God called Adam out of worry, saying, "How are you not in your position? What happened to you? Why can't I feel your presence in the Garden?"

After God judged man, he placed cherubim and a flaming sword flashing back and forth on the east side of the Garden of Eden to guard the way to the Tree of Life (Genesis 3, 22).

Have you asked yourself where the Cherubim came from? I know that God is infinite in his power, and he could have swiped his fingers, and those angels would have appeared, but that wasn't what happened. God took from among the angels accompanying him, his entourage to guard the Garden.

In other words, whenever you see an angel or angels, find out from them what kind they are. If they tell you, you can easily know either that God has a message for you or that he has come on earth to pay you a visit, an encounter.

Don't get me wrong, when you are doing a ministration, angels may show up to assist you, bringing gifts and good tidings, but if you ever have God show up at your meeting, unimaginable things happen.

A perfect example of when God was absent, and an angel was there to announce his absence, was during the death and resurrection of Jesus of Nazareth. The Bible narrates the incident surrounding Jesus of Nazareth's resurrection in the book of Mathew 28: 1-6. Mary Magdalene and the other Mary went to the tomb of Jesus to anoint him. There was an earthquake, and an angel of the Lord descended from heaven, rolled the stone, and sat on it. The angel said to the two women, "Do not be afraid, for I know you are looking for Jesus who was crucified. He is not here; he has risen, just as he said."

This testimony alone should bring awareness to your mind that there are many instances in which God will send an angel to represent him. This validates the fact that the presence of an angel in an environment could either tell you that God is physically present or that he is absent. The fact is that God decides when to physically manifest himself to man, but man can also contribute by seeking God's physical presence.

Guarantee that God is Physically Present in your Life

Moses said in Exodus 33:16, "How shall it be known that I and thy people have found grace in thy sight? Is it not when you go with us? So, we shall be separated, I and thy people, from all the people on the face of the earth." Moses was saying that for there to be evidence that God's presence is with them, there must be a difference between them and the rest of the people of the earth. Moses is a man who has proven what a physical presence of God can do for a man or a people on earth. From his burning bush encounter to witnessing the plagues in Egypt, until he had this conversation with God, Moses understood that God's physical presence is an encounter of goodness.

The presence of God distinguishes you from everyone else on earth, God's physical presence guarantees that you will have things happen to you differently and will be distinguished from the rest of the people on earth. As God led the people physically as they journeyed from Egypt, The Bible said, "The LORD traveled ahead of them in a pillar of cloud by day to lead the way and a pillar of fire at night to give them light, (Exodus 13:21-22). The cloud covered them, and the pillar of fire gave them light at night. God did this to guarantee their safety as they traveled day and night.

When you look at the entire journey from Egypt to crossing the Red Sea into the wilderness, you will see the immense divine presence of God and how God's physical presence guaranteed their victories, safety, and protection.

Moses' conversation with God in Exodus 33:11 will further enlighten you on this subject. The LORD said to Moses, "My presence will go with you, and I will give you rest" (Exodus 33:14). This means the physical presence of God guarantees your rest; he will protect you from your enemies and secure your environment.

Looking at the book of Deuteronomy 23:14, God told his people the importance of keeping their environment clean; God walked through their camp to protect them and ensure their victory over their enemies was guaranteed.

Part of the way God fought for Israel was by pushing through their enemies to a place of defeat. The hand of God supernaturally draws your enemies to the point of defeat. They will suddenly realize that they are at the point of defeat without knowing how they got there. The presence of the LORD guarantees you victory over your enemies. You are assured to be the last man standing at the end because the presence of the LORD is with you.

Chapter Five

You

A Carrier of the Presence of God

Man on Earth is a representative of God; as a representative of God, he must act as a god on Earth. That is God's plan for man from the very beginning. When man was created, God gave him charge over the Earth and everything he created and placed him in the Garden to do as he commanded. (Genesis 1:26-27, 2:15-17).

For a man to represent God very well on Earth, he must align himself with God and become the manifestation of God on Earth. In other words, for man to represent God very well, he must be a vessel and a carrier of God's presence, which I call the Kingdom of God. Man is a conduit of a spiritual presence, be it a conduit or the carrier of light or of the dark world.

Satan requires a body to manifest his plans against humanity on Earth because no demon can manifest on Earth without a body. Someone has to bring his agenda into play; that someone is known as a conduit or a carrier.

When I began to pray for God to reveal himself to me and attempt to focus on the actual Image of Jesus Christ, I began to see myself being transformed into the same image as written in 2 Corinthians 3:18. The more you focus on Christ, the more you become like him; this is the true nature of Jesus Christ, his ability to influence you into becoming like him. It is the most beautiful thing that can ever happen to you as a man on Earth.

The presence of God makes all the difference; it changes any situation. Moses cried to the Lord, saying, "If your presence does not go with us, please take us not up from here" (Exodus 33:15) because he understood that God's presence changes everything. Moses understood the importance of God's presence and how this presence divided the Red Sea, drowned the Egyptian armies, rained Manna from heaven, and sprung up water in the desert for Israel.

The presence of God is potent and makes everything possible. You cannot carry God's presence and not make a difference in the world. You cannot experience God's presence and remain the same. There are people who, when they appear, God appears. In Exodus 33:9, Moses entered the Tabernacle, and the cloud, which represented God's physical presence, descended.

There are certain people God chooses to carry and manifest his physical presence. This set of people can change the atmosphere; when they appear, it becomes the atmosphere of Jesus, as a songwriter rightfully said. This set of people cannot enter your environment without your environment noticing their appearance or visitation.

What am I trying to say? Certain people show up in your environment, and the atmosphere changes to adapt to their presence. It becomes an atmosphere where anything is possible, where miracles can quickly happen, chains break, and bonds are set free.

Usually if you are one of this kind, you will notice strange things happen when you are in an environment. You will have to study yourself properly to know that you are the reason why strange things are happening to your environment or the environment you find yourself in. It means you have become a conduit to the peculiar acts of God; in you is a resting place of God. Just as the Israelites would bring the ark of the Covenant to a location, and changes would take place, 1 Samuel 5:4. Certain people have become that living ark, the walking ark of the Covenant. Hence the reason for the strange things that happen when they are around.

There were many men and women of God, generals of God, who would walk into cities, and by the strange occurrences, the town could tell who was around; the strange occurrences became their signatures. Though I believe these Generals were chosen by God to become the conduits of his presence, they also contributed to the level that God deposited himself in them.

What am I trying to say? Whenever God desires your body as a vessel, he would expect certain level of separation from you. Your life becomes strange; you will suddenly realize you can't do things that others would do freely. You can't walk around or be seen in places where regular people would be seen. The city where you live will become a dangerous one for people who practice witchcraft or Satanism.

The word of the LORD came to Elijah the Tishbite when he hid himself in a cave while running away from Jezebel. The LORD said to him, "Go out, and stand on the Mount before the LORD" (1 Kings 19:11). This scripture says there are specific locations on earth where the physical presence of God is concentrated, thick enough to give you an encounter, to change your situation, and to break your chains. God instructed the Prophet Elijah to present himself there for an encounter.

Moses the Prophet was also instructed by God a few times to appear before the LORD on top of the Mountain. And God told Moses to ensure no man or animal would come around the same Mount. Do you know what God said? He said least they are consumed. In other words, the Mountain was too dangerous to certain people and creatures but was not for Moses, the servant of God. (Exodus 19:12-13, 20-21). It then tells you that it is strictly by election and grace that God choose this set of people as a conduit of his physical presence.

Please don't get me wrong; as children of God, we are all carriers of the presence of God to a certain level. Jesus dwells in us by his Spirit, the Holy Ghost, but there are certain of us who the LORD has chosen to deposit himself to the maximum level as much as we can contain. Apostle Paul confirmed this when he said in 1 Corinth 3:16 that we are the temple of God, and that the Holy Ghost lives in us.

Usually, if you are a vessel that God has chosen to pour himself into in a very solid form, you must comply with his regulations. He gives instructions that you must obey so that he can progressively walk with you.

Chapter Six

When the presence of God is Absent

Jesus Praying the Cup Away

Let me start with this statement: if there is one who ever feared most about the absence of God, it was Jesus at the Garden of Gethsemane. His fear wasn't that of physical death but that of spiritual death, which is a permanent separation from the presence of God the Father. What he feared most was separation from the father as a son. Yes, Jesus was full God and complete man, but in that Garden, his total percentage of God was taken away from him, and he was left with a total percentage as a man. What does this mean? I am saying the Holy Spirit left Jesus once he became sin at the Garden of Gethsemane. A total replica of what happened to the first man created in the image of God, the man Adam.

What Jesus struggled with the most in the Garden was the Holy Spirit leaving him; he wasn't sure what to expect as a man without the presence of the Holy Spirit. Remember, the Holy Spirit descended on him at Baptism, and everything he did from then up until the Garden of Gethsemane was led by the Holy Spirit. After the Holy Spirit separated from him, Jesus sweated blood, a sign of gross anxiety disorder. That's why he kept praying, Father, let this cup be withdrawn from me if possible. He was already feeling the departure or the withdrawal of the presence of the Holy Spirit.

Suppose you watch what happened at the Garden of Gethsemane in Luke 22:42-43, Jesus mentioned to his disciples what was ahead of him many times as the cup of the wrath of God, the significance of the death of the cross. He never imagined the Father's love and presence being taken from him. Jesus had been meditating on what it would entail to drink of the cup of the wrath of God, which was why when the two sons of Zebedee and their mother presented him with a request of positioning in heaven, his response to them was if they were able to drink of the cup he was going to drink. (Mathew 20:22).

The Bible said that Jesus was asking the Father to take this cup of fury from him, but Father's presence was not there anymore. Father had already withdrawn from him.

The significance of the absence of God here means that his prayer would not be entertained, God had already turned his back to him because at this point, he had become sin and God could not stand that sight of iniquity placed on Jesus of Nazareth.

Let me clarify further: when Jesus entered the Garden at Gethsemane, which was a shadow of the Garden at Eden, God the Father remembered what happened at the Garden in Genesis chapter three and how man was separated from his God because of sin; immediately, Jesus became sin, he became the replica of Adam and was separated from the Father.

When Apostle Paul talked about the first Adam as a living soul and the second Adam as a quickening Spirit in 1 Corinthians 15:45, he was referring to the death of the first Adam, who died spiritually when he sinned, and the redemption of the second Adam, who had to die physically to redeem the first Adam spiritually. Jesus was slain physically before the foundation of the earth before he spiritually redeemed the physical man.

God's inability to entertain Jesus's prayer at the Garden of Gethsemane was a sign that God's presence had departed. Isaiah 59:1 reads, "Surely the arm of the LORD is not too short to save, nor is his ear too dull to hear. But your iniquities have separated you from your God; your sins have hidden his face from you so that he will not hear…" That means that sins hinder the answers to your prayer. In other words, when your prayers are not getting attention from God, find out if you are praying from a location or place of iniquity.

Though the angels came to minister to Jesus at the Garden of Gethsemane, the presence of God was gone. Whenever you see an angel, as I said earlier, one of the things it signifies is the presence or the absence of God, depending on the kind of angel.

Do you remember when God told Moses that he would refrain from leading them? When God threatened to withdraw his presence from the people of Israel because of the hardness of their hearts? What did God say to Moses? God told Moses, "I will send an angel to go before you…I will not go up with you, for you are stiff-necked people" (Exodus 33:2-3).

God was saying he would not physically go with the Israelites, not that he would not be aware of their movements. God led the people physically; he walked with them as a pillar of cloud during the day and a pillar of fire at night, so God's reactions were physical when the people angered him. He was walking physically with them; even though they couldn't see him, they saw his shadow, represented by the cloud and pillar of fire. The presence of God is so physical on the earth, but only those in tune with his Spirit can see him.

To reinforce or confirm what I said, God was physical with the Israelites when they came out of Egypt; I will take you to the book of Deuteronomy 23:12-14, where God told the people of Israel as part of their rules in the camp, to have a place outside the camp designated for toileting. He also told them to bring equipment for digging so that they could dig dirt to cover their waste afterward.

Do you know what God said and why he gave them such instructions? Deuteronomy 23:14 says it all. "For the LORD your God moves about in your camp to protect and deliver your enemies to you. Your camp must be holy so he will not see anything indecent among you and turn away from you. You know, the day I stumbled into this in the Bible, I was amazed; I was flabbergasted; how can God give a specific instruction such as this regarding human waste? It tells you that God is detailed and pays attention to even tiny things. Suppose he can pay attention to the number of hairs on your head (Luke 12:7) and how much more the big things. The information you just read should convince you that when God chooses to be physical with you, everything you do matters to him.

As I was saying, the presence of an angel sometimes signifies that God is not in a location, not that he is not aware of the situation; he is aware of the situation or location because he is Omnipresent and omniscient, but he can choose to withdraw from a location physically. You are better off with God's presence than seeing his angels. For some of you who are constantly yearning for angelic visitations, as supernatural as that could feel and be, the Presence of God is the best thing that can happen to anyone.

Partial Obedience

The reason God's physical presence was limited and Stalled God's Plan for Abram

Let us consider Abraham's life and how he stalled God's promise from materializing on time. Many preachers and teachers have taught that God promised Abraham, but this promise didn't happen until he became old.

Well, I will go through the scripture with you, the way the Holy Spirit did with me, and we will find out how Abraham delayed God's promises by not following instructions strictly. God is strict when he gives you instructions, and don't think he doesn't know what he is saying or doing when he asks you to do something.

The LORD said to Abram, "You get out of your country, away from your kindred (descendants of common ancestors), your father's house (your familial place, location, and territories), to a land (another earth, location) that I will show you, Genesis 12:1.

God literally told Abram to get out of his entire lineage, his familial place and territories to another location, a new earth that only God would show him.

When God is interested in making you a concentrated place or conduit of his presence or power, as many would say, the first thing he does is call you to himself. Whether you respond to it or not is totally up to you. Usually, you will not know how to react to it, so he will also have to teach you by His Spirit how to respond to his calling.

When God calls you to himself, you are usually entangled with many things, which may not make it easy for you to get up and go. You may be a people person or in a very lucrative job or place before God calls you to himself. As a side note, God doesn't call idle people. Most people he calls are always busy running their businesses or their fathers' businesses, just like Father Abraham and Elisha.

Abram was busy with his father's household, known for his organizational skills and ability to lead. But he was in a very dangerous territory, a place of concentrated idolatry.

He was from the Ur of the Chaldeans, a heavy idol worshipping community. God was saying to Abram, I need you to become a conduit of a generational blessing, which was in the form of a heavy presence of God. Still, before that could happen, you will need to separate yourself from your environment, your people, and your job. It would have been tough for Abraham to effectively carry out God's instructions in that idol-infested location.

God usually waits until you carry out the specific instruction before moving forward. And God waited until Abraham was separated from his father's house, which Lot represented, before moving forward with him.

As I said, Abraham stalled God's promise by not following the basic instructions that God gave him. When God called him, he told him to leave his kindred, his father's house, to a new place or location. God didn't tell him the specific location, but he needed him to move out of his father's house and from his kindred (community).

When Abraham finally obeyed God's instruction, he took his nephew Lot, who also brought his own group of people, the same people God was trying to separate Abraham from. If you notice, from the time Abraham departed from his father's house with Lot and Lot's household, God didn't speak to him again until he had an issue with Lot and finally separated from him (Genesis 13:14).

Lot was a significant distraction in Abraham's life and calling because he did not truly obey the initial instruction God gave to him, which was to get up and go, leaving everything behind. In the book of Genesis 14:14, Abraham heard that Lot was in trouble and was a prisoner of war; Abraham took his men and went to war because of him. Until Sodom was destroyed, Lot continued to influence Abraham's life and calling to the point that God had to negotiate with Abraham before he could destroy Sodom and Gomorrah, the reason being that Abraham still had that attachment to Lot, even though he was separated from him, he still had him in his heart.

Whenever God calls you, he gives you a very clear unambiguous instruction, which is usually what he needs you to do to get you to the next level, but like I said earlier, it's up to you weather you obey the instruction or not. And the earlier you obey, the better for you in the progression of God's purpose for your life, delayed obedience is said to be a form of disobedient.

Natural Disaster

The significance of the Absence of God in an Environment

There are certain things that separate people or an environment from the presence of God, and it is called sin. When people choose sin over God, he withdraws his presence, and what they will experience is a natural disaster, which is the man of sin, the devil. He is a natural disaster because he is the origin of sin. The Bible says the earth was without form and void (Genesis 1:2). Have you asked what created the void and disaster on the earth? It was the presence of the man of sin, Lucifer the devil when he was cast out from heaven. Anywhere he appears, you see a natural disaster;

that is his nature. When God withdraws his presence from a place, what you will have is called a natural disaster.

Nature's response to the absence of God in an environment can be devastating; it is called a Natural disaster. In a place where the presence of God is limited, a different presence takes over the rulership of that environment. When you look around countries and cities that have experienced natural disasters, most of them have been named after a person, depending on their character. When a storm misbehaves, such as devastating or killing people, its name is retired, and a new name is added to the list.

Natural disaster can therefore be defined as the absence of God in an environment; it is that atmosphere where God is not. One thing we must understand about God is that he is always in control. He had entrusted the earth to humanity (Psalm 115:16). When God gave us authority over the earth, he did not abdicate his role as the creator; he delegated the responsibility of managing the earth to us. All the challenges the earth faces, including natural disasters, are a result of our attempts to remove God from our environment.

Opposing forces have influenced the people of the world to try to keep God away from the earth he created. However, it is not possible to do that; the earth suffers as a result of the consequences of man's actions, which mainly involve neglecting or rejecting his maker. If you study the Book of Genesis chapter 1:2 very well, you will understand one major thing: God's absence and the presence of someone else called Lucifer. Lucifer, in his fallen state, is corrupt and disastrous. The Scripture said, "The earth was without form and void: and darkness was in the face of the deep." The earth was formless and void because of the presence and mismanagement of another force. There is nothing God creates that he does not sustain, including the earth.

We understand that God is omnipresent because he is everywhere. I agree with that narrative, but there is another narrative about God that we have yet to understand. It is the absence of God in an environment that gives birth to an opposition called natural disaster.

David said, even if I make my bed in hell, there you are (psalm 139:8); it means that God is everywhere. But God is also a presence, and if he is a presence, it means he can withdraw himself from a place. The same David begged God not to take his presence, the Holy Spirit, away from him (Psalm 51:11).

Thus: wherever God withdraws his presence from, something else takes over, and it is called a natural disaster. The presence of God is what keeps the whole creation in place, he chooses to concentrate his presence in an atmosphere, and at certain times, he also chooses to limit his presence in an environment. This, my friends, is what we call a natural disaster. When God is concentrated in an environment, he sustains life and creation, but if for any reason he feels that his presence is no longer warranted in an environment, he withdraws from there, and natural disaster takes over.

When God is present in your life, you see his presence, which comes with benefits. His presence subdues the force of nature and keeps it in place. But if God decides to withdraw his presence from you, these significant benefits disappear, and you will experience a natural disaster. Certain people are also carriers of God. When they enter an environment, you will experience exactly what you would experience as if God came physically because they carry God. This means they have God in a concentrated form. Their presence is a testament to the power and influence of God. When they enter your proximity, you will experience things like God came to be with you, these kind of people are very few on earth.

Moses encountered God in a burning bush, which was burning but not consumed, and he became a god unto Pharaoh. It means that what God gave to Moses in that burning bush encounter is called a concentrated presence of God. Have you asked why the bush was burning but not consumed? God's presence-controlled nature and the bush was burning but not consumed because God's presence sustains every creation.

The same miracle happened to the Hebrew boys in the burning furnace. God presented himself before the fire, and the presence of God in that environment stayed the natural components of fire. God, who is called "All Consuming Fire," subdued the fire in that burning furnace.

When the presence of God is withdrawn, what you have is a natural disaster, which was what happened to Egypt in the Red Sea. God's presence separated the people of Israel from the Egyptians, and what they encountered was a natural disaster.

When God decides to confront us, he doesn't need to raise a hand. All he has to do is withdraw his presence, and nature itself will rise up against us. This is not a punishment, but a natural consequence of the absence of God's sustaining presence. It's a reminder of the vital role God plays in sustaining both humanity and nature.

Chapter Seven

How Creation and Demons Respond to The Physical Pesence of God

The first thing to ask yourself is, what does the presence of God bring to an atmosphere that makes it very difficult for demons to inhabit? The word of God says that our God is a consuming fire (Hebrew 12:29). This scripture refers to God's presence because God's anger burns and consumes. The first time this scripture was given to the people of God, Moses was told to warn the people against idolatry of any form, because he is a jealous God and a consuming fire; especially when it comes to dealing with strange gods. This is a testament to the awe-inspiring nature of God's presence, a presence that demands our utmost respect and reverence.

Whenever God manifests in any environment, his presence is undeniable. It's not a matter of 'taking over 'but rather of the creation recognizing its Creator, which naturally elicits a profound response.

Consider the mountains like Mount Sinai, that God's presence passed by or descended upon. Mount Sinai was renowned as a place of divine encounters, as there was a tangible manifestation of God's presence there. Moses experienced most of these physical manifestations on top of that

Mount. God would often descend, then summon Moses to meet him there, or would send a prior invitation to Moses about their meeting on top of the mountain, as recorded in Exodus 34:2, "Be ready in the morning, and then come up on Mount Sinai. Present yourself to me there on top of the mountain."

In Exodus 19:18, Mount Sinai reacted to God's presence by smoking out. The Bible says the LORD descended upon the Mount in a fiery form, and the mountain reacted by becoming a smoking furnace and quaked vigorously. When the people of Israel witnessed the physical presence of God upon the mountain in Exodus 20:18, they saw it in the form of thundering and lightning and heard the voice of trumpets. How did they respond? They withdrew and stood at a distance. Why? Because when the true presence of God manifests, only the pure, those who are free from sin and idolatry, can stand before Him. This is because God's physical presence is like the purest light imaginable, purifying the atmosphere. And this purification is what people respond to by either fleeing or standing afar off.

When Elijah was called up to Mount Horeb, where God was to meet with him, the Bible said the LORD passed by, and the wind cut the rocks into pieces, then an earthquake quaked the mountain, and then fire appeared (1 Kings 19:11). This sounds like what Moses and the people experienced on Mount Sinai; He is the same God.

The essence of telling you the whole story is to bring to your awareness that God's Physical presence does come with physical manifestations; the environment, the atmosphere, and creations, including man, have a way of behaving when God is physically present in an environment.

How Demons Respond to
God's Physical Presence

To truly consider how demons respond to the actual presence of God, we will look at Jesus's life and how the devils answered him. By understanding this, the next time you enter an environment and begin to hear loud noises, commotions, or quarreling, check if the environment is responding to the true presence of God that you carry or if God is standing before you.

After his temptations in the wilderness, Jesus of Nazareth entered the temple, a synagogue, to preach the gospel of the kingdom. Before he entered, it was a calm environment, with no commotion. However, once a man possessed by a demon saw Jesus, the Bible records that the man cried out in a loud voice, saying, 'What do you want with us, Jesus of Nazareth? Have you come to destroy us? I know who you are—the Holy One of God!' (Mark 1:24). This incident illustrates how demons react to the presence of God.

The first thing to ask yourself here is, who spoke? Was it the man or the demon? Once you answer this question correctly, you can now say very clearly whether it was the man who saw Jesus or the demon.

What I am trying to say in effect is this: when a demon or an evil spirit habits someone, the man behaves, sees, and speaks differently from the natural man. The original man's vision is distorted; they view things from the demon's perspective under the influence.

Therefore, there are certain people you have been trying to convince to see things from the right perspective, but they cannot, until you cast out the devil influencing them. This is where the transformative power of God's presence comes in, offering hope and faith that even the most distorted perceptions can be corrected.

The demon spoke to Jesus and responded when Jesus commanded him to leave the man. The Bible states that the devil shook the man violently, then left him (Mark 1:25). This is another example of a physical manifestation in response to the presence of God.

Do you remember in the old testaments when God descended on the Mountains, they reacted by renting in pieces and smoking fire? Now, have you asked yourself why, when people cast out demons, the demons react by becoming violent? It is because of the presence of God that they experience. Our God is a consuming fire; this is a reality. Whenever the actual presence of God is present, your environment, the atmosphere, and even the people around you will react either positively or negatively.

I have observed numerous times, when there is a significant change in my environment, particularly on days when the presence of God is palpable. I notice how the birds react, the trees sway, the wind picks up, and even my children and husband exhibit unusual behavior. These are all tangible changes in the environment that occur in response to the presence of God.

Initially, I didn't know why things would suddenly turn that way, but as I grew in God's presence, I became more aware of some of these behaviors. People sometimes pick up a fight with you because they are reacting to the presence of God that you have become. You may need to know that you should not take it personal with them because they are also under the influence; the demons are indirectly reacting to the presence (the Jesus) they can see in you. Just cast out the demons, and they can see clearly.

Chapter Eight

Can The Presence of God Depart From You?

Why and How the Glory Departed from Israel

Whenever the next generation's survival or succession is questioned, and no man can stand for the people, the Glory of God departs from that generation. Hence: the Glory departed from Israel because there was no provision for the next generation. You realize that at a particular time in Israel, God was quiet on them and allowed them to go into slavery because there was no man for God to walk with. No intercessor was found to stand in the gap for the people.

The Lord God will depart until He finds a man to stand as a prophet or a judge over his people. The Lord's departure here means a withdrawal from his physical presence. Whenever the progression of the new generation is in question, Glory departs; whenever a nation or a people lack plans for the next generation, Glory departs. God is generational and loves continuity. And whenever his plans for the next generation are stalled, he either departs from the people or searches for another man willing to continue from where you stopped. It becomes the end of an era for that people.

Many men and women of God have lost touch with God because they stalled God's plans for the next generation or made it their agenda. If you focus on the next generation's priority, you will continue to see God's Glory in your life.

In Eli's case, the Glory departed from Israel because his house could not produce the next generation of priests. As a result, the word of God was scarce in Israel until the next generation of priest and prophet was produced in the person of Samuel. (1 Samuel 2:1-20, 3:1-20)

Moses lost focus when he began to doubt God's plan for the next generation, which caused him to lose the promised land. Some people said that the law couldn't take Moses to the promised land, and that's why Moses died without reaching it.

I beg to differ here because if you look at this scripture very well, you will understand that God's purpose for Moses' was to lead the people from Egypt to the land flowing with milk and honey, and God does not make promises he does not fulfill. The question should be whether Moses agreed with what God had promised him.

Let's consider the discussion between Moses and God when he spoke to him face to face as a man speaks to a friend. The first thing Moses did wrong was bring Joshua to attend his meetings with God. In Exodus 33:1-11, Moses went into the Tabernacle, where he was meeting with God, and he brought Joshua with him. In the process of this discussion, Moses had to go back to the camp, but the Bible didn't tell us why Moses had to suddenly go into the camp while he was still talking with God face to face. What is mysterious is this: when he suddenly left to return to the camp, he left Joshua behind.

And when he returned, the Bible said he started negotiating with God concerning who God was going to send with him. What Moses did here was very dangerous, called relegation of duty. And I believe it's from his familiarity with God. He was becoming too comfortable with God, that's the reason he brought his servant Joshua to attend a meet with God. What does that tell you? This God always warned Moses, saying, "Do not allow anyone come close to the Mountain...least I consume them, Exodus 19:21. But he brought Joshua with him, meaning he was already looking at Joshua as his replacement.

As I said earlier, Moses became too familiar with God, and he began to allow Joshua to join his meetings with God. In that process, he began to negotiate with God concerning Joshua. In Exodus 33:12 when Moses returned to the Tabernacle, where he spoke with God and he asked God who he would send with him. This was a man that God had led from the burning bush up until now, and he suddenly asked God who will go with him? Now he needs another company apart from God. He asked God this question because Joshua was in the Tabernacle with him, and he wanted God's approval of Joshua.

Now, when you examine what God said to him in Exodus 33:14, you will understand that Moses was really asking God to consider Joshua, his servant, as one who would also lead the people, which was the beginning of his problem.

God said, "My presence shall go with thee, and I will give thee rest". If Moses was asking for who would accompany him on this journey, God said, I will accompany you, but if you want rest from this assignment, I will give you rest.

In other words, God is saying, my presence is enough to lead you and the people through, why asking for another company? God reminded him about his presence which had led them out of Egypt, and the reason for this conversation was because God had considered sending an angel with them instead of leading them, because of their stubbornness, Exodus 33:2-3. Many times, men of God have preferences on who will succeed them in ministry, regardless of God's plan for them and the next generation. In the case of Moses, God granted him his heart desire, Joshua succeeded him.

Moses was one man that influenced God, he caused God to change his mind many times concerning the Israelites. God wanted to destroy the people a few times when they rebelled against him, but Moses stood in the gap for the people. I must accredit this to Moses; he is one of the greatest intercessors that ever lived. As a man that was abused few times by the people he led, they tried to stone him few times, and tried to physically beat him up, but he continued to plead their matter each time he appeared before God. That is a heart of Gold, a heart of an intercessor.

In Numbers 14:1-22, we could see how the people planned to return to Egypt, they suggested to pick up a leader who could lead them back into Egypt rather than follow Moses forward, and when Moses and his brother Aaron tried to stop them, they decided to stone them. If not for the Glory of God that physically appeared before the Tabernacle, the people would have stoned Moses and anyone who tried to stop them from returning to Egypt, Number 14:10

Moses again interceded for the people, because what God came to do was to kill all the people then start another generation with Moses, but Moses stood between God and the people, he negotiated with God concerning the people, numbers 14:12-20. A different man of God would have agreed with God to slay the people and move on considering what the people had done to Moses, but Moses stood and interceded for them. But notice that each time Moses said something to God concerning his people, he listened.

to Moses and does what Moses says. Could this have amounted to Moses's familiarity with God, a man who made God change his mind multiple times? A man who twisted the hands of God to favor his people. God said to Moses after he interceded for the people of Israel, "I have pardoned according to thy word" (Number 14:20). Who on earth would touch God and make him reason with him the way Moses did? It is a great thing to find favor before God, it is called Grace.

The familiarity with God caused Moses the promised land, and not because he received the law from God. This familiarity continued until he acted irrational before the presence of God. Let's dig deeper into the book of Numbers 20:7-29. God spoke to Moses and Aaron, his brother, when the people murmured against them and almost beat them up again because of their thirst for water, saying "Take the Rod, and gather the assembly together...speak to the Rock...and it shall give His water, and you shall bring them the water, and give to the congregation, and their livestock" Number 20:8

What do you think Moses and his brother Aaron did? I would hold Moses more responsible for this action, more than his brother because he was the one who had seen the Glory of God the most, he had become too familiar with God.

Moses took the Rod before God and gathered the people rather than obeying God's instructions; he scolded the people and struck the Rock twice. He decided to act in place of God this time, which was counted to him for unbelief. Do you remember God said, "The rock will give his water?" This Rock God referred to as a "HE" meaning the Rock was a person. Moses and Aaron were commanded to speak to the Rock, but Moses struck the Rock twice. God was offended, he was not happy with them, Numbers 20:10-12

First, God wanted Moses and his brother Aaron to do exactly what he told them, "Speak to the Rock," so that the Miracle of speaking to the Rock and the Rock releasing his water would become a sign for the people to believe that God is indeed in their midst, and that God is walking among them. It would have been the final Miracle to help the people acknowledge God's physical presence.

That was what God was trying to say when he said, "Because you believed me not, to sanctify me in the eyes of the children of Israel...Numbers 20:12. The Rock was a representative of the presence of God among them, but Moses had become complaisant, which is one of the most dangerous thing that could happen to man who has become too close to God. Whenever you get to the point of trying to replace God in people's lives, God withdraws his presence, just a warning sign, to prevent them from encountering problems with him.

Remember, Moses also had an anger outburst when he returned from being with God for forty days and forty nights? The anger outburst led to the crashing of the first stones of God's Physical handwritten laws. Moses crashed the stones, and God looked away, but he took note of it. There were many other things Moses did not do as God had instructed, but obstructing God's plan was the limit Moses got to with God.

God outwardly judged Moses and Aaron his brother, Aaron died immediately after this, because God would not want him as a priest anymore, so he was stripped off his priestly garment and he died, Numbers 20:26-29.

The lesson is this: Never take the people God assigned you to lead for granted. God has a way of disciplining his own children, and unless he assigns you that place, you should be careful how you treat the people of God, he takes it personally.

In conclusion, Moses didn't enter the promised land because he became familiar with God, starting from when he brought Joshua into the Tabernacle during his meetings with God (Exodus 33:11) to when he did things differently, away from God's instructions. His decisions to do things differently from God constituted disbelief before God.

The Bible says that after the Generation of Moses and Joshua, another generation emerged that didn't know the Lord. And the reason they did not know the Lord was that the fathers neglected their responsibilities (Judges 10:2).

Whenever a new generation springs up who have no knowledge of God or his past deeds, it signifies one major thing, the fathers failed. That was the sin of Eli, which he paid a terrible price for. God said he warned Eli about his son's, but Eli did not reprove his sons regarding their iniquities. God keeps records of how you treat the next generation, because he is a generational God; and his presence can be withdrawn from you for ignoring his plan for the next generation.

Jesus and the Withdrawn Presence of God

Jesus made a very controversial statement because people always say, "He will never leave you, no forsake you," not considering that to be a conditional statement. You know Jesus of Nazareth; even though he was the manifestation of God in the flesh, he also needed God's complete presence to function. Jesus was full of the Holy Ghost, his life after being baptized in Jordan. The Spirit descended on him and remained with him, making his environment a spiritually saturated one. He lived constantly under the shadow and under the wing of the glory of God the Father. That was Jesus' spiritual and physical habitat, a place where his source of life was drawn from. When Jesus made the above statement, he was not bragging; he was stating his reality.

Considering what Jesus said in John 8:29, "And he that sent me is with me: the Father hath not left me alone; for I always do those things that please him." In my understanding here, Jesus said, Father has not left me because I always do what pleases him, a conditional statement that could not be overemphasized. It brings you back to the question: Can God leave you? If God the Father cannot leave you, why is Jesus talking about God leaving him? God is everywhere, as we know because he is Omnipresent. However, there are certain locations where God takes preference and has deposited himself significantly into; one of them is the man he created. What God is to man is what man is to his environment, so can God leave an environment? Can he withdraw his presence from an environment?

Jesus was in the garden of Gethsemane, and he was troubled greatly because the presence of God had departed from him. The lack of the presence of Father will surely bring an anxiety attack to anyone who is used to communing or living in that very presence. To Jesus, God the father withdrawing his presence here was as significant as death itself. Its significant can be likened to what happened to Adam and Eve at the Garden; God withdrew himself from them, which was the death he had promised Adam when he said "For in the day that you eat of it, you shall surely die"(Genesis 2:17). Death here, represented a separation from the true presence of God, which was also Adam's true habitat and reality. In other words, whenever the enemy wants to have a say in your life, he will cause you to do something that will make God withdraw from you. As a child of God, the enemy has no say whatsoever in your life, because your habitat is in Christ, who is in God, so how can the devil have a say? There is a wide gap between you and the enemy, he is constantly under your feet, but he is also always looking to influence you into a separation from your true habitat into a place he can have a voice in your life, an action which is totally depended on you.

At this point in Jesus' life, the presence that he was used to, was taken away from him, because at this time he was also made a sin, and everything Adam did was placed on him, which caused that separation to happen between him and the father. For the first time, he had a feeling of a great vacuum, an emptiness. This was why he kept going back and forth to his disciples to help him pray, maybe God could hear their own prayers. He was going back and forth to see if anything could be done to help him. Jesus here was like a fish out of water, fishes we know need water to breathe, and if you take a fish out of water, it dies after some time.

Jesus was sweating blood, which medically is called hematohidrosis, or hemidrosis: a condition which occurs from the rupture of the capillary blood vessels that feed the sweat gland. This medical condition is medically proven to occur under conditions of extreme physical or emotional stress. He was struggling for air, he was asking for his natural oxygen, which was the presence of the father. Cutting that off was as significant as death, in other words, Jesus died first in the garden of gethsemane even before he got to the cross. Don't get me wrong, the death Jesus died happened first spiritually when the father separated from him, his death on the cross, was a physical manifestation of what had already happened.

Jesus was sweating blood at the garden of gethsemane (Luke 22:44). It was such an intense feeling of anxiety, and panic attack that made him run back to his disciples to see if they could help him out. It is a very dangerous thing to be locked out of the presence of God, and if you have ever been exposed to the divine presence of God, you will understand what Jesus felt at the garden of Gethsemane, he couldn't hear from God anymore because his presence was withdrawn from him.

While on the cross dying, before he gave up the ghost, Jesus cried out, "ELI, ELI lema sabachthani?" which means "My God, My God, why have you forsaken me?" this word forsaken is a Greek "egkataleipo" kat-al-i-po, it means to abandon, leave one behind, to desert someone.

Jesus was deserted and abandoned by his own Father to suffer shame because of the man he created, to redeem man back to himself. When Jesus was hanging on that cross, dying, all kinds of sins were listed all over him. Every form of sin that man could ever commit was placed on Jesus. On that cross, he was a murderer, he was an adulterer, a thief, name it, yet he knew none of those sins. (2 Corinthians 5:21). Father looked away, that he may be able to look towards you and me and have a relationship with us today.

Jesus, who was so used to constant communion with God, was dependent on the Father. For once in his life, he felt the father's absence. God was silent. His silence signified his absence. In John 5:19, he said, "…I do what I see my father do." In other words, he needed the father for every step he took, and for once, he didn't have the father to guide him. That was a terrifying time of his life on earth.

Most of the time, when you don't hear from God, it means one thing: He is speaking, but you are not hearing, or he moved away from you. Though he can still see you, his presence has been withdrawn from you. Don't be deceived, many people have experienced this, some who were humble enough acknowledged it and wept unto God who restored mercy to them. Others just moved on with their Ichabod. Silence from God is a terrible feeling. Some people who have been in this situation can tell you, it is not pleasant at all.

King Saul and the Withdrawn Presence of God

King Saul is the best person you could ask what it feels like to be separated from God. When the Spirit of the Lord, which signified the presence of God, departed from him, the Bible said he could not hear from God anymore. (1 Samuel 28:6). God did not answer him by dream, Urim, or the prophets; that was a terrible state. Anytime you stop hearing from God, it may be significant of one thing: God may have withdrawn his presence from you. How can God speak to you when his presence is no longer with you?

King Saul was in a very bad state, where God did not only desert him, but also cut off communication with him and his prophets. The Bible tells us that God used to speak to King Saul, and once his presence departed from him; his means of communication was also taken away from him, 1 Samuel 28:5-6. What does this really tell you? Whenever the presence of God departs, his voice also departs; many can't hear from God anymore because his presence has departed from them. Anything that will cost you the presence of God, you should avoid. You should treasure the presence of God so much because his absence or the withdrawal of his presence from you, will cost you a terrible level of anxiety. Therefore, many who have been left behind, try to pressure up, and if it doesn't work, they end up negotiating with the devil for power.

I know a famous scripture in Hebrews 13:5 where Paul said, "Let your character be without love of money...for he hath said, I will never leave thee nor forsake thee" KJV. Another translation said, "Keep your lives free from the love of money..." NIV. What is your understanding of this scripture? if your character is without love of money, he will not leave you nor forsake you?

God cannot stand Idolatry; the love of money is Idolatry, and God frowns at Idolatry because he is a Jealous God. Look through your scriptures and see how God responds to Idolatry, He said in Exodus 34:14 "For you shall worship no other god, for the LORD, whose name is Jealous, is a jealous God" NKJV.

It baffles me how many Children of God claim that God is the same yesterday, today and forever, but their engagements are otherwise. If you believe this, which I do; do you think he has stopped being a jealous God? Will God judge Idolatry less today? If he is the same yesterday, today and forever, he was a just God yesterday, and he couldn't stand Idolatry yesterday, why would He stand it today? Why would He excuse your Idolatry today?

The love of money means you can do anything for money, and that you have become a servant to money. Jesus said you can't serve God and Money, (Mathew 6:24). Money is a spirit, and it is possible to worship money. The worship of money is called Idolatry, it means you have forsaken one to worship another. It means you have chosen to worship an object that was created rather than the one who created it. God is also a Spirit, and you ought to constantly be in worship to God. Don't allow anyone to deceive you; Grace is there to teach you and guide you, and you cannot continue to deceive yourself and believe God cannot withdraw his presence from you and your idols.

Eli and the Withdrawn Presence of God

If you pay attention to the first time Samuel, the prophet, heard from the LORD, the Bible says he went to his master Eli because he thought Eli had called him. The problem was that his master Eli stopped hearing from God because his two sons, Hophni and Phinehas, were sons of Belial, who did not know the LORD and sinned continually before the LORD. And Eli, the priest, did not correct his sons properly. 1 Samuel 2:17.

Eli stopped hearing from the LORD because the LORD withdrew his presence from him, and he couldn't speak to Eli anymore. As I said earlier, one of the signs that the presence of God has departed from you is the absence of his voice; he will not speak, and you will not hear from him if he is not there. But the LORD visited the little boy Samuel and started calling him by his name. When this started happening, he thought Eli was calling him. After the third time, Eli perceived that God was calling Samuel, and he guided him appropriately.

Eli couldn't hear the voice of God calling Samuel, but Samuel could. What a mystery—that two people would be in the same location, and God would withdraw his presence from one and give it to another. What am I trying to say? Eli couldn't hear the LORD calling Samuel but was in the same environment with him. The Bible said that the LORD was standing by Samuel as he was calling him, 1 Samuel 3:10.

The point I am trying to make here is that many have been deceived into thinking the LORD will never leave them or forsake them. If you read that scripture very well, you will understand the reason given in the same scripture why the LORD will not leave you.

In conclusion, the first thing that usually happens to a man or a woman when God withdraws his presence from them is the feeling of restlessness and anxiety, because they can no longer hear from God. If you have ever heard from God, and suddenly he stops speaking to you, it is going to trouble you greatly. That's why David said to God "Cast me not away from your presence, take not your Holy Spirit from me..." Psalm 51:11. Once the presence of God departs from you, Satan comes to oppress you, 1 Samuel 16:14.

Sin, disobedience, or rebellion are reasons God may withdraw his presence from you. If you ever find yourself there, where you can no longer hear from him, it means one thing: God has withdrawn his physical presence from you, and you need to quickly retrace your steps and get back into a place of fellowship with him for restoration. He is a loving God, and his faithfulness drives his mercy towards you.

Apostle Paul said in Romans 6:23, "Should we continue in sin so that Grace should abound?" The Greek word used here is the word "pleonase," which is a word that means to superabound. What on earth can be used to replace the Grace of God? Nothing! And to continue to live your life the way you want, especially in sin, believing God will continue to wait on you, is a total deception. When you sin or live a life of sin, you tell God that what Jesus did on the cross was not enough; that's the true meaning of grace abounding. Don't be deceived; God loves you jealously, but he is a Holy God and cannot withstand sin. Whenever you feel you have missed it somehow, return to his love, repent, and ask for forgiveness. True repentance will lead you to a place of restoration.

Chapter Nine

The Gift of His Presence

The Holy Spirit and Impartation

Many monopolized the gospel and the church of Jesus Christ, trying to make it their personal family business; the body of Christ has become their church, and the members of Christ, their members, thereby making the gospel of the kingdom of less effect.

To you who run from one man of God to another, seeking the laying on of hands because you are desirous of the mantle, have you asked yourself if you have what it takes to carry the mantle? Can you carry the mantle you are running around seeking?

What are you Carrying?

You know Elizabeth, the mother of John the Baptist, was pregnant with something; she was six months pregnant with a baby, and when Mary, the mother of Jesus who was full of the Holy Ghost and Power from the Most High, visited her (Luke 1:35), something was activated in her.

The Bible says that when Elizabeth, the mother of John the Baptist, heard Mary's greetings, the baby in her womb leaped for joy. Do you know why?

That baby was a promise and was supposed to be filled with the Holy Ghost from the womb (Luke 1:15).

When Mary went to the home of Zachariah, the Father of John the Baptist, the promise made to her (Elizabeth) by the same Angel who visited Mary was activated. Mary's presence activated that promise; her presence got John the Baptist and his mother Elizabeth, the carrier of that promise, filled with the Holy Ghost because of the seed in Mary, the Seed of the Holy Ghost.

The problem is that many are running around looking for a man or a prophet to lay hands on them, but they are empty, carrying nothing. What can you activate in an empty vessel?

Let me reveal something that may shock you today: laying hands and impartations are mostly Old Testament methods of contacting the Spirit that a man of God carries. Have you ever asked yourself who laid hands on Jesus, John the Baptist, Peter, John the Beloved, Paul, and many others? The Holy Ghost descended on them, which is why they significantly impacted their generation.

In the Old Testament, God had prophets lay hands on people to raise them to carry their mantles, just as Elijah laid hands on Elisha, Moses on Joshua (Deuteronomy 34:9 & Numbers 27:18), and so on. But in the New Testament, the Spirit of God descends on people. Are you still in doubt? Jesus is a perfect example. After he was baptized, heaven opened, and the Spirit descended upon him like a dove (Luke 3:22).

The disciples of Jesus Christ in the upper room, while in one accord, heard a sudden sound like a mighty rushing wind that filled the room, and then fell upon every one of them as cloven tongues like fire, (Acts 2:1-4). This was the beginning of the manifestation of the Holy Spirit through them.

This represents how the New Testament believers contact the Holy Spirit, it does not mean that the laying on of hands does not work, but if you have nothing in you, the effectiveness is not guaranteed.

Also, When the people of God were gathered unto the Lord in a church at Antioch, the Bible said some prophets and teachers were worshiping God while fasting, and the Spirit of God said to them, "Separate for me, Saul (Paul) and Barnabas for the work I have set for them." (Acts 13:1-3). But because the people were so used to impartation by the way of the Old Testament, they still laid hands on them.

The Spirit of God did not tell them to lay hands on them. It was an Old Testament culture, something the church borrowed from the Old Testament, which has remained. That's why you have many running around all over the places, seeking men of God to lay hands on them, because the people have become so ignorant and lazy. No one wants to pay the price by patiently waiting for the gift of the Holy Spirit to be activated in them. Instead, they are running all over the places looking for mantles to carry; the laying of the wrong hands has destroyed some.

Why did the Bible say that Jesus "... commanded them that they should not depart from Jerusalem but wait for the promise of the Father" (Acts 1:4, Luke 24:49)? Jesus strictly warned his disciples not to go anywhere until they received the Holy Spirit. But these days, many are running around looking for some man to impart what they are carrying, even though they cannot differentiate what the man has.

Can I explain further? Why did Paul say in 1 Corinthians 12:4-5 "There are different kinds of gifts, but the same Spirit distributes them. There are different kinds of service, but the same Lord. There are different kinds of work, but it is the same God at work in all of them and in everyone." He concluded in verse 11, "All these are the work of the same Spirit, and he distributes them to each one, just as he determines."

The Holy Spirit is the one who determines which gift you get, as He desires. It means the Holy Spirit in the New Testament determines who can be imparted with a gift and who will not; it is all the prerogative of the Holy Ghost; he knows you more than you know yourself and determines when you are ready for an impartation.

If you dig deeper into the scriptures, you will notice that most of the laying on of hands was done to heal the sick. That was what Jesus commanded us to do. Jesus laid hands on the sick to heal them Luke 4:40, not to impart spirits to them. When a leprosy man approached Jesus, he knelt before him and begged him for healing. The Bible said that Jesus reached out his hand and touched the man, and his leprosy was cleansed (Mathew 8:2-3).

To appropriate the laying on of hands, Jesus told his disciples to wait on the promise of the Father; if he had wanted us to continue to lay hands on people to impart them like in the old testaments, he would have just laid his hands on all his disciples before he ascended to heaven. Jesus made his disciples demonstrate to us in the upper room as an example of how to receive the Holy Ghost properly. They were all in one accord and praying in faith believing for the gift that was promised them (Acts 2:1-2).

Saul of Tarsus, after he encountered Jesus, was sent into the city. While he was there praying as instructed by Jesus, he saw in a vision where a man named Ananias placed his hands on him to receive his sight, and then Jesus told Ananias to do just that. The Bible says Ananias laid his hands on him, and he received his sight and was filled with the Holy Ghost. Acts 9:3-18.

Why does your man of God lay hands on you, and you get imparted? Because the gift is already at work in you, and you were just ignorant. The laying on of hands can activate the gifts of God in you, that's for sure, but the model and the priority, as Jesus intended it to be, was for you to receive the Holy Ghost the same way the disciples did, to avoid the confusion of today. There is confusion among people running around for mantles even without any substance in them. That's why many have been laid hands on, and still, nothing is working in their lives. It is because there is nothing to activate.

Look well into the word of God. Before God told Moses to lay hands-on Joshua in Numbers 27:18, the word of God said the Spirit was already in Joshua. God instructed Moses to lay hands on Joshua to activate the Spirit that was already in him. It means that the only impartation you can ever receive is the Spirit already in you and not any new spirit. But you can also get imparted with strange spirits if the wrong person lays hands on you.

Apostle Paul said to Timothy, "Lay not hands-on anyone suddenly, neither be partaker of other men's sin" 1 Timothy 5:22. It is because you can easily transmit or receive something when you lay hands on someone that has no power or capacity to carry what you are trying to give to them; many have been laid hands on suddenly, which aided to their destruction in ministry. You can help in someone's destruction by laying hands on them suddenly. It means you must be sure that this person is ready, and the only way you know that is by the Holy Ghost. Also, you can suddenly participate in someone's sin by laying hands on them as well. There are certain people who God has afflicted, if God is not done with them, you may become an accomplice to what God is trying to relieve them of. Just like the case of Saul who became Paul, he was afflicted with blindness for a season by Jesus and was told who to meet when he repented and was ready to preach the gospel of Jesus Christ.

Notwithstanding, the Holy Spirit also watches to see how much you hunger and thirst for the impartations of these gifts, for the manifestation of his gift in your life, and he will guide you through. In other words, when you hunger and thirst after the gift of the Holy Spirit, there are certain things you do which prepares you for these gifts. The Holy Spirit knows when you are ready to receive the gift of the Spirit.

Pentecost

The Influence of the Holy Spirit upon your environment and the people around you

The Miracle at Pentecost was profound in addition to what happened to the disciples; its depth is in the people and the environment around them. When the Holy Ghost came upon them (the disciples), his influence on them, their environment, and the people around them was remarkable.

The Bible said the place where they dwelt had many Jews and many devout men from every nation of the earth, Acts 2:5. And when the people heard the commotions going on around the disciples of Jesus, how they were filled with the Holy Ghost, great multitudes rushed in to see what was going on, and they were dumbfounded. The reason why they were shocked was because everyone who was there heard them speak in their language. In other words, everyone who came to see what was happening to the disciples heard them in their various languages; the people understood the disciples by the Holy Ghost's influence.

That was one of the significant miracles that happened on the day of Pentecost; the Holy Ghost that descended upon the disciples also caused the people in their environment to manifest the presence of the Holy Ghost, which is the interpretation of tongues.

The Bible says, "Every man heard them speak in their languages, "Acts 2:6. How were they able to hear them in each of their various languages? The Holy Ghost also gave them an understanding and interpretation of the tongues spoken by the disciples.

It means everyone who came close to their sphere, their magnetic field, and everyone who came close to where the disciples were on that day, were influenced by the Holy Ghost. That's how they understood and interpreted the tongues spoken by the disciples of Jesus Christ on that day; the whole atmosphere was under the influence of the Holy Ghost.

Not only were they dumbfounded, but they also asked questions, "Are not all these men Galileans? How, then, do we hear them speak our own individual languages?"

They understood that something supernatural was happening to the disciples and them equally, so they asked that question: How were they able to hear the blabbing sound coming out of the disciples in their languages? It confounded them that they understood and interpreted the disciples' tongues. That is what the manifestation of the Holy Ghost is; everyone who comes under your sphere gets under that influence, and they get sucked into the heavenly arena. And they begin to manifest the gift of the Holy Ghost.

Let's consider what Prophet Samuel said to Saul, "when you leave this place, you shall meet a group of prophets when you arrive at Gibeah of God, they will be coming from a high place of worship, they will be prophesying, and you will prophesy" 1 Samuel 10:6.

Do you know what this means? Saul went forward, and as he came before the prophets who were prophesying at Gibeah, the Spirit of God influenced him, and he prophesied 1 Samuel 10:10. Do you know why Saul could prophesy? He came under an atmosphere, under the influence of the prophetic Spirit, and that's why Saul was able to prophesy.

In other words, when you are a conduit of the prophetic or the physical presence of God, you should be able to look at your environment and know when the Spirit in you is influencing it.

When the disciples experienced the Holy Spirit visitation in the form of a cloven tongue of fire, their environment was also under the influence of the Holy Spirit; the same Spirit made the people understand and interpret the tongues they heard.

Another thing we miss when we read this scripture is what the people heard in their languages. I am believing the Holy Ghost for the ability to hear what they heard on that day. A multitude of them, which were about five thousand, out of which three thousand later gave their lives to Jesus Christ and were baptized (Acts 2:4), were there on that day, and they heard the disciples speak in their various languages; that's the miracle of the Pentecost.

Concentrated Presence of God

Have you ever wondered, why it is that when you shake a man of God with a certain level of concentration of God, or when they lay hands on you, you fall "under the power"?

You are made to fall because the God in them is more potent than your spirit, and you have to bow or submit to what they carry.

The woman with the issue of blood experienced a miracle when he touched the helm of Jesus garment. To Jesus, it was an osmosis; a power that left him, but to the woman with the blood issue, it was a miracle, a healing she had sought for over 12 years, (Mark 5:25-40). Her issue of blood dried up immediately, that is, by surrendering to the higher power, the concentrated level of the supernatural power of God in Jesus of Nazareth

A great example was when the Philistines captured the Ark of the Covenant in the place of battle. Though the Philistines captured the ark, they didn't know what to do with it; they had no place for it. The Philistines didn't have a prior preparation or place for the ark, so they decided to place it in the house of their god, Dagon; that was the closest place they could find for the ark. Their rationale was that the ark was the God of the Israelites, and he should share a room or space with their god, Dagon. 1 Samuel 5:1-2.

When they woke up in the morning, their God had fallen under the power in reverence to the ark. Dagon bowed to the ark. But on the second day, Dagon also fell with its head and hands broken off. 1 Samuel 5:3-5.

You know, before you carry that level of God's presence, you must be prepared for it. Moses was prepared for the heavy presence of God when God told him to take off his shoes because the ground, he was standing upon was holy. Have you ever wondered why Moses is called to the top of the mountain where there is a heavy concentrated presence of God, but the rest are warned not to come near the Mount, lest they be consumed? Exodus 19:21. Have you asked yourself what would have consumed them? It is the presence of God. When God's presence is concentrated in a location or a person, it can mean miracles for some and death for others.

Let's get this correct: God told Moses to tell the people to wash up, clean their clothes, and keep away from their wives because he (God) wanted to visit them. This means that the level of iniquity or uncleanliness in you reduces the manifestations of God to you. What it means is this: Moses had a level of righteousness or purity that made him attain and stand face-to-face with God and not be consumed.

Let me tell you what happened to Moses at the burning bush when God said to him, remove your shoes for the place where you are standing is holy ground, Exodus 3:5. What made this place a holy ground was the concentrated presence of God in it, God was physically standing there, that's why the bush was burning but not consumed. The presence of fire is the manifestation that God is present in this case; Our God is a consuming fire (Hebrew 12:29).

Therefore, Moses was initiated into the concentrated presence of God before he could get closer to God. First, God told him not to come close; you know why? Because then, Moses was so unclean, and if he had come closer, this concentrated presence of God would have destroyed him rather than cleansed him. It then tells you one thing: it is still by-election that God chooses who will carry him in a concentrated form, "Many are called, few are chosen" (Mathew 22:14).

That was exactly what God meant when he said to Moses, I will have mercy on whom I will have mercy on, and I will have compassion upon whom I will have compassion, Numbers 33:19.

In the New Testament, as I said earlier, in Acts 13:2, the Holy Spirit spoke to them while they were worshiping to separate Paul and Barnabas for the work, he had called them to do. The carrying of the concentrated level of God's presence is not for you to walk around or to show off; it is for the work of God.

The gifts manifesting in the lives of many are by the will of the Holy Spirit; 2 Corinthians 12:11. It is the Holy Spirit who determines who will carry the gifts of prophecy, healing, working of miracles, etc., the same way he determines who will carry the concentrated presence of God. When you have this concentrated presence of God, most of, if not all, the gifts of the Holy Spirit will be seen in full manifestation in your life.

The Holy Spirit is the presence of God; he is the manifest presence of God the Father, and when you see him in fullness without measure, you are said to have God in a concentrated form. Jesus while on earth manifested the fullness of the Spirit; God the Father gave him his Spirit without measure, John 3:34.

The Physical Presence of God

Can it be Seen?

The physical presence of God can be seen, those who have the privilege to see this physical presence call it the move of the Spirit. The shadow that moves with God can truly be seen by the physical eyes. These shadows that represents the physical presence of God could be seen throughout the Old Testament especially during the time of Moses. The shadow and the pillar that moved and walked around them came was a replica of the physical presence of God.

God at a point told the people of Israel to handle their toileting well because he walked around their camp to secure their victory, Duet 23:12-14. The physical presence of the God who defended Israel was so present among them. Also, in the book of Numbers 14:10, when the people gathered to stone Moses and his brother Aaron and those who tried to stop them returning back to Egypt, the LORD appeared and stood in the Tabernacle, and the whole congregation saw the LORD as a shadow of glory. That Shadow was a physical representation of God.

Again, in the time of King Solomon, after the dedication of the temple, the bible states that the LORD descended in form fire to consume the sacrifice, and the glory filled the temple that the priest could not get into the temple. That shadow that the people experienced is the physical presence of God as could be seen, (2 Chronicle 7:1-3).

There is a certain level of the presence of God that you will have; when people see you, they don't see you; they see God. Daniel 3:20-27. King Nebuchadnezzars ordered for the Hebrew boys to be thrown into the fiery furnace when they refused to bow before his image and worship him. When he investigated the fire, not only did he see the three boys who were thrown into the fire walk around freely amid the fire, but he also noticed that they had a company, Jesus, who was walking around with them in the fire.

Do you know what is impressive here? He was not only able to see the fourth person walking with them, but he made a baffling statement: he said the fourth man is like the Son of God. How did he know what the Son of God looked like? Jesus hadn't even manifested. What was he trying to say? The word son of god used there is Elah and deity, the same word as Allah in Islam, as used in Aramaic. In other words, King Nebuchadnezzars was a Muslim and was accustomed to the things of Allah. And when he saw Jesus walk among the Hebrew boys, he took him to be the son of Allah. It also means that another in the likeness of Mohamed had also existed before he came to be.

What I am saying is this, Mohamed was not the beginning of Islam; it existed in Egypt even before the birth of Jesus of Nazareth. And just as Islam disagreed with Jesus as the Messiah, they also worked against the salvation of the Jews. What am I trying to say? Islam was and is still the religion in Egypt; that was the religion Pharoah practiced.

85

My point here is that Allah had existed even before the time of Mohamed. Allah is a spirit being, a deity, just like one of those gods, those other countries who warred with Israel worshiped.

You have Baal, the Hindu god that looks exactly like the epe god that some parts of the Yoruba land worship. Briefly look at the image of the Hindu deity and the Yoruba epe gods. They are the same gods, though their names are different. The idols are the same, regardless of the century or time. They may have different names, but they are the same idol.

Finally, Jesus of Nazareth is the physical expression of God the Father, and whenever you see Jesus, you have seen the tangible presence of God, which is his physical presence.

In the Last Days

The Lord God said to the prophet Joel, "It shall come to pass afterward, that I will pour out my Spirit upon all flesh" Joel 2:28. But before we consider this statement, look at what Peter said when he quoted this scripture in the book of Acts 2:16-19. Apostle Peter, on the day of Pentecost, needed to clarify the curiosity of the people trying to imagine what had suddenly become of the disciples of Jesus Christ and why they were speaking in diverse tongues.

Peter, trying to clear the air and their speculations that they have been drinking, said, "But this is that which was spoken by the prophet Joel. And it shall come to pass in the last days, saith God, I will pour out my Spirit upon all flesh: and your sons and your daughters shall prophesy, and your young men shall see visions, and your old men shall dream dreams: And on my servants and my handmaidens, I will pour out in those days of my Spirit; and they shall prophesy…"

When you look at the book of Joel, the word "in the last days" is not in it because revelation is continuous, and no prophet knows everything because God speaks when he has someone willing to listen and communicate what he is saying. The Lord sent these words to his people through the prophet Joel, telling them what would become of them, but he didn't tell them when these words would manifest. It brings me to a significant statement: when God speaks, pay attention to his words and timing. God can tell you something today, and because God is timeless, it is for you to verify the timing for which what he spoke is to be expected.

In other words, through the prophet Joel, God's words were for a specific time, which Apostle Peter called "the Last Days." God promised us his Spirit would fully manifest in the last few days.

Now, let's get back to the Book of Joel regarding what God planned for his people in the last days. Poverty is an evil inheritance; whenever God wants to move, you first experience an introduction of surplus, abundance, and wealth. The word of God calls it the Glory of God.

The Glory of God precedes his manifestations, which is his physical presence. The condition of the people before the word of the LORD was spoken by the prophet Joel was that of lack, famine, and impoverished lives. The fields were in great waste, and the land was in mourning because of the condition of the people (Joel 1:10). A Situation where not only the people were suffering, but the land and the animals in the land were also suffering from lack of Pasture.

The manifestation of the Spirit of God, as promised to us in the last days, will lead to the manifestation of the supernatural life of God, not only in your physical body but also in your environment. It means your natural body becomes supernaturally qualified to do supernatural things by the presence of the Spirit of God upon it. The Spirit of the Lord takes over the control of your physical body, quickens it, and makes it a supernatural body. When your flesh receives this ability, it can do unnatural things as Jesus did. He walked on water, went through walls, and appeared to people in different forms; your natural body will manifest these abilities and more, just as Jesus had promised.

It is to prepare you for where you are going because in the new Jerusalem, as stated in the Book of Revelation 21:1, John the Beloved said he saw a new heaven and earth. The processing of your flesh is to prepare you for the supernatural feeling of newness. Your ability to experience the supernatural in your flesh will give your spirit the hope to prepare for the newness.

When the Spirit of the Lord possesses your flesh, your mortality becomes immortality; this is also what you need to prepare and to experience rapture. When the Spirit of the Lord is upon your flesh, you can easily walk upon water and through walls, and no devil will limit you. This is what the Church of the Lord Jesus Christ needs now: an outpour of the Spirit of the Lord, a quickening Spirit that would empower us to prepare for the return of Jesus Christ.

God is territorial, anywhere he enters he takes over. He is the God that created the heavens and the earth, and when he enters any space on the earth, he dominates it, the earth feels his presence. He is the God that fills all in all, (Ephesians 1:23). He fills the whole earth that he created, and everything in it, what an awesome God!

Chapter Ten

The Anointing of
The Holy Spirit

Does it Decrease?

The word pray without ceasing is a spiritual command given to us by Jesus Christ. To carry out this commandment of praying without ceasing, you must create a perfect environment for the Holy Spirit to thrive. The Holy Ghost is the Spirit of Prayer, and just like Apostle Paul said in Romans 8:26, we do not know how to pray well or what we must pray about, but the Spirit of God will help us with intercessions through groaning that natural words cannot interpret.

The Holy Spirit is patient in working with us in our weaknesses, especially with prayer. The Bible says in Romans 8:25, "If we hope for what we do not see, we wait patiently," meaning that while we wait for our expectations to be met, we develop patience.

Then, the next verse (26) says, "Likewise, in the same manner, the Holy Spirit helps us with our weakness." Have you asked yourself in what manner this verse was saying? It says that in the same manner, we wait patiently for what we hope to appear; the Spirit of God patiently helps us in our weaknesses. In our prayerlessness, the Holy Spirit patiently waits for us and helps us work it out to the point that we groan with words that cannot be uttered. It means that the things we say when we pray are too dangerous to be spoken out, so we groan.

If you can make your life conducive to the Holy Spirit, you will carry the fire and prayer anointing. Through this anointing of prayer, you can climb up the ladder and be translated to the level that all eyes will be on you only if you understand what prayer is and how to pray effectively.

The Price You Pay

There are prices you pay for the anointing you receive to be established in your life. The anointing you receive is the ability that God gives to you to manifest the kingdom of heaven.

You often look at great men and women of God and desire to be like them, but will you be willing to pay the price they pay daily to manifest such power?

We look at the likes of Elijah the prophet, Moses, Samuel, the Apostles of Jesus Christ, and other Generals in the Kingdom, and we fast and pray for God to give us such anointing as theirs. We are not open to seeing the prices they paid behind the scenes that gave them access to such manifestations of the presence of God by the Holy Spirit. Though the Grace we call "the anointing" is from God, they made significant sacrifices to keep the anointing they received from dissipating.

No one knows Elijah's parents; all we know about him is that he is a prophet, a Tishbite who just appeared and displayed God's supernatural manifestation in a heavy way (1 Kings 18). We also read that God asked him to do certain things, which he did, leading to the destruction of the prophets of Baal.

The point is this: Elijah also stayed in the mountains, was fed by Ravens, and did not have a particular place he called his own. Elijah had no wife or children and was entirely dedicated to serving God. If you ask to be like Elijah, are you also considering making the sacrifices he made? Will you pay the price to sustain the anointing you are desiring? Because once you receive this anointing, there are situations that the anointing would also attract.

Another example is the life of John the Baptist, as the Bible says in Luke 1:17, he came with the anointing and the spirit of Elijah. When the angel Gabriel delivered the message to his father Zachariah in Luke 1:17, in verse 15, we are made to understand that John the Baptist, who was to come in the spirit and power of Elijah, should not drink wine or strong drink and shall be filled with the Holy Ghost from the womb.

Now, I want you to see this: John the Baptist, who came in the spirit and the power of Elijah, did not drink wine nor strong drink and was filled with the Holy Spirit from the womb. It then means that the kind of anointing that Elijah had could be defiled or limited by wine and strong drinks. Since John had the spirit and the power of Elijah, he also lived in the mountains, which the Bible called a desert, and there he ate wild honeycomb and locusts and wore only clothes made of camel's hair.

Do you see what I am trying to say to you? As an Elijah or John the Baptist of this generation, which you believe God to be, there are also specific diets you must keep up with and certain liquids you must avoid. Your garments must be made a certain way, and you must be ready to dress a certain way. Do you know why? Because the spirit and the power you receive can only be maintained in a certain way and location. Otherwise, the anointing will not function properly and may not be maximized.

Christ is the most incredible anointing to be desired, but some today prefer to be like the prophets of the old rather than crave the footsteps of Jesus Christ on earth; he is a perfect example for us as believers.

The anointing you receive from God must be taken care of by you, the recipient of the anointing, because there are conditions to maintain that level of anointing. To manifest in the power of Elijah, or John the Baptist, and be able to defeat the prophets of Baal, you must also be able to stay up in the mountains, which could mean you locking yourself up inside a room in prayer and maintaining a specific diet for a while. It would help if you did not desire an anointing, which you cannot keep as a prophet; it will destroy you.

Moses and the Price he paid for the Anointing

In the life of Moses, he paid a great price for the anointing of a deliverer, which he received at the burning bush. Moses, who negotiated with the LORD about his inability to carry the anointing that the LORD was offering him, was almost ruined by that same anointing. His failure to make it to the promised land resulted from the intricate nature of that anointing he received from the LORD at the burning bush.

Moses agreed to what God said after negotiating with God at the burning bush, which is also a Mount of God called Horeb (Exodus 3:1). He took his wife and children after he told his father-in-law Jethro that he was going to check on his people in Egypt. I see this action as valuable wisdom for Moses, who never told his father-in-law Jethro what his encounter with God was and that he was the leader who would facilitate the deliverance of his people from Egypt. He would have had a problem with his father-in-law over taking his sons and his wife, Zipporah.

Where am I going with this? Moses, after he took his wife and his sons, left for Egypt, and we suddenly read that God wanted to kill him at the entrance of the inn, a hotel where he lodged with his family. No one said anything about the reason why God would suddenly want to kill a man who was already on his way to the mission he was called for. Exodus 4:24.

The Lord clarified what happened while Moses was in the inn.

After he was commissioned for his journey, Moses took his wife and his two sons and went into a hotel, and God was offended by that. Moses had just been initiated into the burning bush to be in proximity to God. Proximity in the sense of being face to face with God and not being consumed, he received an ability to stand close to God, who is an "All-consuming Fire" and not be consumed. Moses' ability to go up the Mount of the LORD, which others could not get close to, was because of this anointing (initiation) he received at the burning bush (Mount Horeb, the Mount of God).

To God, Moses did not understand the intricate nature of the anointing he received. It is not the kind of anointing that you carry into the inn and go about sleeping with your wife. You were set off on a mission, thinking about sleeping with a woman was a very dangerous thing at this point in his life, and because Moses received a dangerous anointing, it almost killed him.

Let me explain further: when Moses left the burning bush (Mount Horeb), God physically followed him. God followed him back to when he spoke to Jethro, his father-in-law, picked up his wife and kids, and entered the inn with his family. It was what happened at the inn that God was offended at. How could you keep God physically waiting while you are busy sleeping with your wife? God's firstborn Israel was in anguish in

Egypt, and when he found Moses and anointed him, he chose to go into an inn with his wife.

There are certain kinds of anointing that you would receive from God that would elicit certain occurrences in and around you. One thing you must do is to be prepared for those occurrences. There are certain things God cannot stand when he is face to face with you; it could mean death to some people who offend the anointing, such as the earth opening to swallow some people, and leprosy to others who accuse you even if they were right.

God expected Moses to leave his family with his father-in-law and continue the mission. It did not mean he would have lost his family; God wanted him to get the Israelites out first, then pick up his family and proceed to the promised land. Do you remember that Moses later married an Ethiopian woman for whom his brother Aaron and his sister Miriam spoke against? Yes, he was allowed to be married because even God came down to defend him on that matter and called him the faithful (Numbers 12:7). Moses was allowed to be married, but sleeping with his wife at that point was a disdain to that fresh anointing which he had just received from God.

Many men and women do not know that part of the price to pay for carrying the presence of God, such as the kind Moses and other patriarchs did, is a sacred living and abstinence from sexual relationships.

By the Grace of God, I understood that Moses told the people in the camp not to go into their wives because of what happened to him at the gate of the inn (Exodus 19:15). He understood what could happen to a man who appears before the LORD unclean or unprepared: It can lead to death; it is that presence of God that consumes.

Also, by grace, I understood that part of the reason Satan contended with an arc angel, Michael, for Moses's body, as written in Jude 1:9, was because of this anointing that Moses received to be in proximity with God. Moses's anointing gave him the capacity to see the part of God that Lucifer was not privileged to see, Exodus 33:23. Lucifer wasn't called an anointed cherub for fun; he received this same anointing that Moses received and came in close contact with God Almighty; he is called the anointed cherub that covereth because he was also in close proximity with God. Do you remember Lucifer also walked on the Mounts of the LORD? We were made to understand that in Ezekiel 28:14, Lucifer walked up and down the Mount of God amid stones of fire; that's the only way you could be in proximity with God Almighty, your ability to contain or withstand heavy fire, which was what Moses was initiated into in the burning bush.

Jesus As Our Example

When you look at Jesus's life and that of his disciples, you will understand why he functioned exceptionally in his anointing. He was always in the mountains or desert, praying or teaching people. People around him noticed that he stayed more in the desert than in the city; they would go to the desert to look for him (Matthew 14:13).

First, the Bible made it clear that immediately after Jesus received the Holy Ghost, he was led into the wilderness to be tempted, Luke 4:1-2, which I call proving the anointing. Any anointing you receive must be proved or tried, which proves your ability to sustain that anointing. That's precisely what happened to Jesus and what happens to everyone who receives an anointing from the Lord. It is your responsibility to find out the anointing you received from the Holy Spirit and what you must do to take better care of that anointing to maximize it in the kingdom of God.

At one point, Jesus also told his disciples that "this kind goeth not out but by prayer and fasting" (Matthew 17:21). This means that the level of power or anointing needed to deal with that lunatic or legion demon that disturbed that boy can only be sustained by a life of prayer and fasting. That's what Jesus was indirectly telling his disciples.

You cannot have an everyday life where you sleep with your wife every night, eat three square meals, pray only when you want to, and then rise to cast out certain demons such as the legion. Yes, you received that anointing, but to manifest it to the maximum capacity, which is the capacity of driving out up to two thousand demons at once, you must live a dedicated life of prayer and fasting and consecration. Don't forget that at this point in the lives of the disciples, they could barely fast, and some of them would sleep off in the place of prayer, Mark 14:37.

Please be wary of how you live when God releases the anointing you have prayed for. The Holy Spirit is always here to help you. Make Him your friend, and you will never go down. Your anointing will not decrease or depreciate. Walk with the Holy Ghost, and you will maximize your anointing.

Jesus of Nazareth

How God anointed Him with the Holy Ghost and Power

As a conduit of the power of God, you must be anointed, first with the Holy Ghost and with power. Jesus, even though he was the physical expression of God the Father, still needed to be anointed; this part of him is called Christ.

When you look at this part of the scripture in Act 10:38, you would not but wonder what Apostle Peter was trying to say there. When did God anoint Jesus of Nazareth? After John Baptized him? When then, did he receive power? We all read how immediately he stepped out of the river Jordan, the heavens opened up to him, and he saw the Holy Ghost in the form of a dove and lighting, descend upon him; he also heard a voice speak to him saying, "This is my beloved son in whom I am well pleased." Matthew 3:16-17.

This was the voice of God the Father confirming to Jesus his sonship. John also testified that he saw the Spirit descend and remain with him, but only Jesus heard the voice. That was what kept him through his temptations in the wilderness. You cannot stand certain things alone until you encounter God.

According to Matthew, Jesus saw the Holy Ghost as a dove and lightning, but the writing in Luke 3:21 did not mention lightning. However, we believe Matthew because we have also read Jesus' description of the fall of Satan in Luke 10:18, where he also used the word lightning. I am trying to say that unless you have encountered God for yourself, you will not fully testify to what his power feels like because what you see and hear confirms who God is to you. Also, you cannot have the power of God without the Holy Ghost, and to exhibit power without the Holy Ghost it's witchcraft.

To be a conduit of the physical presence of God, you must carry God in a concentrated form, and the only way to do this is by encountering God yourself. Any man you see manifest the presence of God physically is a product of an encounter, meaning he has met with God face to face. Moses met with God face to face and carried his presence. Jesus, God in the flesh, still needed to encounter the Father face to face; that's why he continued to say, I do what I see my Father do (John 5:19).

To be a conduit of God's physical presence, which means manifesting God as He is, you must see what God does. How do you see God without spending time with Him?

I am trying to say that you must learn how to date God so that you can carry his presence.

Jesus would walk away from everyone, including his disciples, and go to the top of the mountain to spend time with God the Father. His disciples called it prayer, but Jesus called it abiding.

This is why he told those who believed in him, "If you continue in my word, then are you my disciples "(John 8:32). Anything you focus on; you can transform into. Jesus is the word of God made flesh, and for you to become part of him, you must abide in his word.

Jesus also told his disciples to tarry in Jerusalem until they encountered power, Luke 24:49. Why did he say that? Because he wanted them to become conduits of the power of God so that they could manifest God in the flesh. It was physical evidence when they eventually received the Holy Ghost and Power. In the book of Acts 2:2-5, the people saw the Holy Spirit descend on them, the same way he descended on Jesus when he was baptized, which means that the power of the Holy Spirit is physical. You encounter him (power), you must be seen with that power; it's not something you can hide.

Chapter Eleven

The Blessing

A Manifestation of God's Presence

The presence of God is a currency through which we can access true riches and wealth. Naturally, as a carrier of the presence of God and a child of God, you are guaranteed a manifestation of true blessing and wealth. This manifestation will come from God's wisdom and power to acquire wealth.

Apostle Paul said, "The wisdom we access as the children of God is uncommon and not the wisdom of this world, and because it's not the wisdom of this world, it's foolishness to the natural man." He concluded that a person who the Spirit of God spiritually accesses can judge all things because this person is spiritual (1 Corinth 2:7,9,14-15).

The blessing we received in Christ Jesus is supernatural and spiritual. God blessed us with it in heavenly places and Christ Jesus (Ephesians 1:3). The problem is one's ability to convert the blessing or to transfer the spiritual blessing to a physical or earthly realm.

The earthly blessing came from Abraham because we are all blessed in God's covenant with him (Genesis 12:1-3). It means no National blessing went by any other means except the Abrahamic covenant.

As children of God, we inherited spiritual blessings in Christ Jesus, but these blessings are in spiritual form and heavenly places. And only those who are spiritual can access these blessings in Christ Jesus. For "who knows the things of God except the Spirit of God" (1 Corinth 2:11). Your ability to access the Spirit of God is the access you have to the thoughts of God, which is the unsearchable wisdom, a currency to the wealth in God.

Galatians 3:29 says, "If we are Christ's, then are we Abraham's seed, and heirs according to the promise. "And to know that we are Christ's, we must have his Spirit in us. (Romans 8:9). What promise is Paul talking about here? No other than Abrahamic promise. The promise made to Abraham by God in Genesis 12:1-3, where he was told, especially in verse 3, that by him will ALL the nations or families of the earth be blessed.

Once you can access the Abrahamic blessing by faith, this promise will manifest in your life. You will begin to see those who curse you become cursed, and those who bless you become blessed.

Paul in Galatians 3:29 says that if we are in Christ, we are the seed of Abraham and therefore heirs unto that promise of being a blessing, and through us shall also all the families of the earth be blessed.

Why are we not manifesting this promise then? If you look at that scripture very well, you will understand what it says: we are Abraham's seed and heirs to salvation. Meaning we are in seed form. In other words, as a seed, you will have to fall to the ground, die, and germinate, and then you can form roots and branches.

Galatians 4:1 says it all. If you are children in spiritual things and the spiritual realm, you are like servants, and though you are the lord of all, you are under tutelage and guidance until God decides. Please permit me to say that the one who decides when you are qualified for the physical manifestations of the promise of Abraham in your life is the Father of all blessings.

Poverty

An Evil Inheritance

According to the Father of Faith and Blessings, poverty is an evil inheritance, so let's explore the true meaning of that statement. The LORD said to his people in Joel 2:25, "I will restore the years the locust, the cankerworm, the caterpillar, and the palmerworm had eaten" by giving plenty in abundance to the point of satisfaction. God promised his people a restoration that would come in the last days. The reason he is going to do this is because he has seen the years that were taken away from them. For them to experience the fullness of his spirit in the last days, they will need to be in a different atmosphere called satisfaction. This atmosphere, he also said, comes with the knowledge of God.

Experiencing the true knowledge of God and that he is a provider also comes with personal encounters. God emphatically stated that he would be the one to manifest to his people, so much so that they would all have personal knowledge of him as a provider and a restorer. Afterward, the people will experience a glorious recovery, and shame will be taken away. It means that shame replaces something in your life, the blessing, which is what father Abraham called an evil inheritance, an inheritance from other sources but God.

The Spirit of God cannot manifest fully in an atmosphere of lack and pain because poverty already rules that atmosphere, and the people will not perceive him well. Have you ever asked a poor person his interpretation of God? Poverty beclouds a man to the point that he loses the ability to perceive right and interpret well. That's why I said earlier about God's statement that his provision and restoration will lead the people to the proper knowledge of him.

This statement means that your knowledge of God in a place of poverty is limited, and you cannot say you have a true knowledge of God if you have not encountered his provisions and restoration.

How do you tell a person with nothing to eat that God is good? To them, the true statement of this would be to give him to eat before he would understand that statement in a realistic form.

What I am saying is that if you meet a hungry person and try to give them the gospel, you will be wasting your time and energy. But if you meet him, feed him, and then present the gospel to him, the possibility of receiving this gospel you just preached to him is very high because you demonstrated the goodness of God to him by feeding him.

Jesus demonstrated the good news to the people in multiple places, who in turn consistently sought after him. At one point, he pointed out that they sorted him out because of the food he provided them (John 6:26). The people ate and were filled.

What I am saying, in essence, is that the poor receive the gospel differently and will not have the true knowledge of God until they have come out of the atmosphere of poverty, which father Abraham stated was an evil inheritance.

God said to Abraham, get out of your environment, your atmosphere, and forget about your father's house; go to the land I will show you because I intend to make you an origin of a blessing, not just to your generation, but the whole nations on earth, Genesis 12:1-3. Have you ever asked why God told him to get out of his heritage entirely? That's why I am writing all these to convince you that poverty, like Abraham said, is an evil inheritance.

God looked at Abraham, his environment, his atmosphere, his father's house, and his kindred, which included his ways of believing and reasoning, and realized Abraham could not have a true knowledge of him (God) if he stayed in that atmosphere of poverty. He needed him to move away from his poverty-infested atmosphere to understand God correctly.

Do you remember Abraham getting out but taking Lot, his nephew? That affected him and how he related to God until Lot separated from him. When Lot eventually separated from him, study the choices Lot made and how he ended up. That is one effect of poverty on the mind; it leads to bad choices.

Poverty, especially lack, is a strategic weapon the enemy uses to weaken the people of God; he uses it so much because he knows that for them to experience God truly, they would need to have a true perception of who God is.

Apostle Paul said it so well in Hebrew 11:6: without faith, it is impossible to please God, but first of all, to try to please God with your faith, you must believe that He is..." And I ask, how do you get a man lacking and impoverished to honestly believe and have faith to the point that it pleases God if you have not demonstrated what it means to have God?

I am saying that to demonstrate that God exists, you give the poor and hungry something to eat. That's the first gospel they would hear before anything else. That's why Jesus demonstrated this to his disciples: how to preach the good news gospel indeed. When one of his disciples told him to send the multitude away so they could fend for themselves, Jesus said, feed them, Matthew 14:15-21. Could you imagine if Jesus had sent them away hungry after teaching them about the good news without demonstrating what he meant by the good news? In other words, the poor and hungry will not receive the gospel well without a demonstration of the goodness of God by feeding them.

God said his Spirit will be poured out upon all flesh. Do you know why the LORD promised to release his Spirit upon all flesh? Their mortal bodies will be quickened and converted to enable them to live a life of wonder, a supernatural life on the earth. God said he wants to show some wonders in the heavens and on the earth (Joel 2:30), but these wonders can only happen when the people of God are restored, with the outpouring of the Spirit of God; this is what will bring the wonders to the heavens and on the earth.

Do you remember I said earlier that father Abraham said poverty is an evil inheritance? When you read the book of Luke 16:19-25, the parable of the rich man and Lazarus. Here, the Bible said that there was a certain rich man who dressed in purple linen, had each day filled with joyous splendor, and lived an affluent life on earth, and when he died, he went to hell. On the other hand, Lazarus lived at his gate in poverty, want, and hunger. As a result of his malnourished state, he developed sores all over him, which the rich man's dogs would come to lick. When Lazarus died, he was carried into Abraham's bosom.

Have you asked why was Lazarus carried, or better, what was the need for Lazarus to be lifted by angels to Abraham's bosom? The word carried there is the Greek word "Apophero," which means to bear off, lift, or carry forth. Poverty affected Lazarus so much that his spirit was limited, his spirit was so weak and unable to get out of the grave where his body was buried. His spirit was so weakened by his poverty while alive that he had to go through spiritual resuscitations by angels to get into Abraham's bosom.

What am I saying? I am saying that poverty can also affect your spirituality as a child of God. I will tell you why I said so; it is out of what I have been told by the Spirit of God and out of experience that I can stand firm on this matter of poverty affecting your spirit.

My Supernatural Encounter

How Poverty Limited my Access into Paradise

Somewhere in 2021, I had an encounter when I finished praying one night. I was taken to a city filled with white buildings in this dream. The gate was white, and the whole city and the walls were as white as snow. The people at the gate were also wearing white, though there were different skin colors. They were all clothed in white raiment.

Upon entering the city, even from afar, I heard worship songs coming from the clouds, and I was looking for where the songs were coming from. When I looked, the same song was being sung everywhere, it was such a harmonized worship. Even though the worship songs were coming from the clouds, the songs were so close, as if the people worshiping were so close to me; it was such an angelic atmosphere. As I got to the gate, I was greeted by many who stood there, and I had to remove my shoes and go through the security system as if I was going through the airport.

After I went through the gate, I was met by another group of people who were so polite and smiled at me. They welcomed me with cheers on their faces, but I only recognized one familiar face: a lady who attended the same church with me at that time. She was among those at the gate smiling at me.

While they were all happy to see me, I was so different; I wasn't smiling because I was suspicious of everyone. Even though the heavenly music welcomed me, I was still suspicious of everyone. That's what poverty would do to you; it makes you overly conscious and afraid.

When one of the men approached to explain to me where I was entering, as I was being welcomed, he started by telling me about the mansions I was looking at. He told me they belonged to the saints, though some of them were uncompleted. This man told me that the reason I was there was because it was time to start building my mansion.

Outrightly, I remembered my mortgage, house, and other bills. I turned to this man and told him that I had a mortgage that I was paying off and couldn't afford another one. You noticed what happened to me here? The poor living on earth influenced my spiritual state of mind.

The man continued with a smile and gently told me that I would not need to pay anything for this mansion; all I needed to do was qualify. He said I only needed to give them my name and other information for the qualification process. He said my qualification was being a believer in Jesus Christ, and once they put my name in the system, the system would generate the location of my mansion.

As he was finishing up his explanations, I turned around. I didn't want to proceed further. I told him I was not interested in giving him my name to run my credit; I was afraid he would run my credit. I told him that I already had a mortgage and didn't believe I would qualify. My poor state also affected my credit, so I did not want anything else on my credit.

He tried to convince me to give it a trial, but I didn't believe him; all I had going through my mind was how much I owed on my mortgage and other bills. I walked out and sat on one of the rocks by the gate.

While I was walking back to the gate, I saw a famous man of God exiting one of the mansions from my far right. Then I said in my heart he should qualify for a mansion in this kind of city because he has money. Immediately I said that I got out of the city and woke up.

Child of God, do you know what happened to me? When I woke up that morning, I began to question my spirit about the meaning of this dream. The Spirit of God told me I had just visited paradise. It was an opportunity to see my mansion in heaven and see how I was doing spiritually. Still, I refused to go in because my physical and financial state also affected my spiritual state. I felt so bad, but I sought God for a turnaround.

You know what I am telling you is a very known fact; poverty which also relates to lack of food to eat in the case of Lazarus, can affect your body to the point that your spirit can also become crippled. Let me give you a physical example: have you ever deprived your physical body of food for days until you begin to feel your spirit weakened to the point you can't concentrate?

What I am saying is this: you can starve your physical body to the point that your spirit becomes uncomfortable. People can die out of starvation because it gets to the point that your spirit is weakened and can depart out of your body because of a lack of sustenance to your body.

I believe this was what happened to Lazarus; he was at the rich man's gate, looking to be fed out of the crumbs that fell from the rich man's table (Luke 16:21). It then means that there was a high probability that he wasn't fed out of those crumbs as often, and because of his malnourished lifestyle, he developed sores that dogs fed off. The dogs licked his sores because either they were hungry too or they were wicked dogs.

In other words, Lazarus was malnourished from lack of food because of his evil inheritance called poverty. He died, and his spirit needed to be rescued also from poverty; that is why he had to go to Abraham's bosom.

Believe me, as I write this, I am made to understand by the Spirit of God that many believers die and are not translated directly to heaven because they have lived impoverished lives, that their spirits would need to be resuscitated to be able to adapt to the heavenly environment; because, as a spirit, you still remember how you lived your life and were tainted by that image of poverty. In other words, your spirit man will need to be renewed to adapt to the atmosphere of heaven, with streets made of gold and solid minerals that your eyes had not seen.

Did you also notice that when the rich man died, he didn't need to be carried? His spirit translated easily because he had enough energy to get into hell. While in hell, the rich man looked up and saw father Abraham and Lazarus by him. Then he requested that father Abraham sends Lazarus to dip his finger in water, then come to hell and drop it into his mouth to cool his tongue, which was on fire.

But father Abraham responded by saying, "Son, remember that thou in thy lifetime received thy good things, and likewise Lazarus evil things: but now he is comforted, and thou art tormented?"

His good things represented the rich man's inheritance, while the evil things here represented Lazarus' inheritance. What was Lazarus' inheritance? Pure poverty was his inheritance. When father Abraham said that Lazarus inherited evil things, father Abraham was saying that poverty is an evil inheritance.

I noticed in the words of father Abraham how he called the rich man "Son."? Do you know why? Because he was a son to Abraham in the sense that every blessing that anyone in any part of the world enjoy is because of the covenant that God had with Abraham. You remember, in the book of Genesis, God promised Abraham while making a covenant with him that the whole earth would be blessed through him (Genesis 12:3).

God told Abraham that all the families of the earth would be blessed through him. In other words, the rich man's blessings were also from Abraham; it was just that he didn't manage it well; he was selfish. You don't go to hell for being wealthy; you go to hell by making money your god, being a fool, because only a fool says in his heart that there is no God (Psalm 14:1). The rich man did abominable things in a corrupt state because he already believed in his heart, that there was no God. What happened to this rich man was out of his own wicked and ignorant heart. He lived as if God did not exist by neglecting the poor around him.

Another thing I want to point out here is the difference between the mindsets of the rich and the poor. While in hell, the rich man's mindset didn't change; he still saw Lazarus as a servant and a messenger. He did not think of it as a big deal, requesting that Lazarus be sent over to hell from Abraham's bosom for a drop of water to cool his tongue (Luke 16:24).

There is such a terrible gap between the rich and poor, and it can be depicted by how this rich man treated Lazarus both when he was alive and when he was dead; the mindsets of the wicked do not change even in death, more so that of a poor man.

There is a wise counsel by King Solomon in Proverbs 4:14-15 that says, "Do not go into or set your foot into the path of the wicked or evil-doers... turn from it, don't even think about it, turn away and keep moving."

Do you know why? "Because the wicked cannot rest until they do evil, sleep is taken out of their eyes until they make someone stumble." Do you know what that means? It is in their nature to do evil things, and they have no control over it because their entire existence is structured to do evil, Proverbs 4:16.

The Spirituality of the Physical

Abraham's Blessing

Everything you see in the physical has a spirituality to it. The things you see with your physical eyes have spiritual origin and sustenance, and nothing exists physically without its spiritual component.

Anything you can see physically has a spiritual representation. The problem is that many people have been blinded to the spirit of the physical things they see. As a person, you are a spirit living in a physical body, why do you think that the things that happen to you are mere physical?

In the Book of Judges, chapter 4, we read a great story about a woman of God and a great warrior called Barak, who warred against the captain of the host of the Canaan army called Sisera. Sisera was a well-known champion with a great multitude of armies. He had about nine hundred chariots of iron, with which he oppressed the people of Israel for twenty years.

When the Israelites cried unto the LORD, he spoke to Deborah, the prophetess who approached Barak. She told him something very significant: Rise to river Kishon, for the LORD will deliver Sisera into your hands. Judges 4:7. It is critical to note the location where the victory was promised. Many times, people miss out on God's promises because they do not understand God's versatility in pinpointing time and location for victories. When you look through the Old Testament, you will notice how specific the people were in locating places where they carried out battles because location determines the success of their battles.

Hence Moses at the Red Sea, Joshua in the Valley of Ajalon, etc. Now, when the Lord speaks to you about anything, try to find the time and the location from him because he is always very specific.

In Judges 4:15, we see where the Bible specifically said that the LORD discomfited Sisera, and as a result, all his chariots and hosts fell to the edges of swords. Though Sisera escaped, he was later killed by a woman he took for safety.

I told you the whole story to bring you to this point. In Chapter 5 of the Book of Judges, we see through the song by Deborah, the prophetess, what truly happened on that day.

In Judges 5:20, we see through Deborah's lenses that those who fought the battle fought from a different realm; they fought from heaven. The Stars also accompanied them in fighting this battle, the Bible said the stars in their courses fought against Sisera.

In other words, when his chariots and hosts fell by the edge of the swords, the stars in their course were also at war against them. That is the spirituality of the physical battle that was fought that day; Sisera and his armies only saw the physical Israel, but it wasn't only physical Israel that fought this battle; the stars and other hosts of heaven were also involved in it.

You know the stars are part of the lights God placed in the galaxy or the firmament to control signs, seasons, days, and years. (Genesis 1:14-16). In other words, when the stars in their course fought against Sisera and his hosts, the stars withheld their lights from them, thereby altering their seasons and days on Earth.

Constantly, people's destinies are being altered by forces from a different realm. Only those who have spiritual eyes can see through people and what is happening to them. No one goes down without being spiritually determined and castrated first. That is why, as children of God, we pray. Prayer lines us up to divine agreement to fulfil God's purpose on earth rather than running a different course as determined by the dark world.

In the battle at the Red Sea, when the armies of Pharaoh realized what they were up against, they decided to turn back and run for their lives. Still, the Bible said that the LORD removed the wheels on their chariots, and as a result of a spiritually mandated act, they all drowned in the Red Sea. Exodus 14:25-27. To the Egyptian armies, they only contended with Israel, but through the eyes of the scripture, we know what truly happened.

The emphasis of telling you the stories above is to bring you to the statement that Abraham's blessing is spiritual. You have been wondering why you have been claiming every blessing and believing, but you haven't seen anything yet. It is because the blessings you received (if at all you received one) are spiritual blessings. The spirituality of this blessing then manifests in the form of physical items you see around you.

If you don't possess the spiritual aspect of it (I call it capacity), the physical element will not manifest. Sometimes, you don't see it manifest physically even after you have received it because there is a force somewhere that has refused that you have it. To some of you, it may be a family member, and others may be the society at large, the dark world.

At this point, you do not need to ask God to bless you; you need to fight and contend with those spiritual forces, and your blessing will manifest physically.

Many believers are in this realm, where God has released many answers to their prayers. To some, these answers are in the form of new jobs and business opportunities, and to others, generational wealth, and inheritance; they see it but wonder why they don't have it yet.

Daniel prayed for 21 days, waiting for a specific answer from God, but the angel whom God sent to bring the answer was prevented by another spiritual force called the Prince of Persia. At last, Daniel got his breakthrough, which is why we know about it. Many people of God do not know that cases such as Daniel's exist today. Daniel 10:12-14

In Genesis, the Bible says that Abraham blessed his son Isaac, but he gave gifts to the children from his concubines and sent them away from his son Isaac. When you read further, Isaac received the spirit of the blessing, and with this spiritual aspect, he was empowered to gain physical wealth.

Isaac carried the spirit of a blessing his father Abraham gave him around; this spirit guided him to the things he did for the physical blessing to locate him. However, God extended the covenant he made with his Father Abraham, which was the spirit behind the blessing, Genesis 26: 1-20. Wherever Isaac went, since he was the carrier of this spirit behind the blessing, the physical blessing would have to find his location. He found himself in Gerar during a famine, he sowed and got a hundredfold harvest. He dug wells and named them the same as his father, only by that same spirit.

That is to say that something controls the seed you sow. The ability to yield a hundredfold is not determined by your action, which is seed sowing; there is some force behind deciding whether you get a yield or not.

Therefore, you can't curse a spiritually blessed man. The spirit behind the physical blessing is the ability and empowerment to make wealth. Do not forget the LORD your God, who gives you power to create wealth,

Deuteronomy 8:18. The spirituality of wealth is the capacity to attract wealth. God gives the actual power to make wealth.

This principle is the same even in the dark world; when people decide to engage in money rituals, they contact the spirit they are given by the agent of darkness through instruction. This instruction holds the spirit of what they have requested together.

Once the instructions are carried out, the spirit enters and possesses them. Once this spirit possesses them, this spirit in them is what magnets monetary opportunities.

If they continue to follow the guidelines appropriated to them, money will continue to locate them because of the spirit of money in them. Once there is a mismanagement of the guidelines given to them, it usually leads to their downfall. Which is generally the beginning of misfortunes until everything they gathered while possessed by the spirit of money departs from them.

JOB as a possessor of a Spiritual Blessing

Job was a man blessed and protected by God; he was God's display of Glory in a physical manifestation. Job enjoyed an open heaven, and divine protection and guidance became part of his nature.

You know, when people enjoy grace, they don't know that grace is priced and paid for by someone. All they do is rise up and enjoy it without being aware of the price that is paid.

The story of Job is a story of one that is said to fall from grace to grass; he didn't know it was grace until he tasted grass. He was a very young, learned man who was adored and admired by both young and old. the

Bible said the secrets of the Lord were upon Job's tabernacle; Job knew God's secrets at his fingertips. When people needed to hear God's wisdom or understand God's secret things, they consulted Job because he had much of it. (Job 29:4).

Not only were the secret things of God with him, but young men of his age would hide from him because he had so much wisdom, and being around Job exposed their ignorance. Elders would stand in awe of the wisdom that came out of his mouth when he opened his mouth. They stood up in honor at the gates when he would pass by. (Job 29:8).

The noble men (princes) who naturally should be the ones to speak at the gate, would refrain themselves from speaking by holding the lips together when Job was speaking. Because of the secrets of the Lord that was with him. (Job 29:9-11).

Men listened to whatever Job had to say, and they would come to him for counsel. People would wait in line to get counseled by Job, because he knew the secrets to everything. (Job 29:21-23).

Job didn't know how much grace he enjoyed because he had the spirit of blessing with him, and God did many things for him.

You know Job could do the things he did as a young man because he had grace working in his life. He could sit among the nobles, the princes, and the elders of the land and stood out because God's grace was in his life.

Job had the ability to rescue the poor who cried out for help and the fatherless who had no one to assist them because he had grace upon his life. Job could gladden the hearts of the widows whose husbands died, leaving them under his care because he had the spirit of blessing with him.

The righteousness Job had on him as a garment to the point that he became the eyes to those who were blind, and feet to those who were lame, a father to those who were in need, and a defender to strangers, and fought against the wicked redeeming their victims from their grip, was because he had the spirit of blessing upon him.

What I am trying to say, in essence, is this: at a point in Job's life, when he was at the peak of the worst adversity from the wicked one, he suddenly realized that the blessing, the wealth, the secrets, were all because of the Grace of God operating in his life.

Job understood at this point in his life that God was commanding his morning for him, making sure that his day of spring was right. God watched over him and the blessings he had. That's why Job said, "Oh! that I was as in the months of old, the days when God watched over me" (Job 29:2). Job understood that it was the light of God that lighted his path, and that's why he was able to walk through the darkness (Job 29:3).

The hedge that Satan accused him of (Job 1:9-10) was the grace that was upon his life; all these things that Job did weren't because Job was able to do them, but because grace was upon his life.

God permitted the devil to test Job by withdrawing the spirituality (the hedge) of his blessing from him. In nine months, Job lost everything except his life. When the spirituality of the physical departs from someone or something, disaster appears.

Looking at the human body, you would believe without a doubt that once a person's spirit leaves the body, the physical starts to decay in a matter of hours.

That's what happens to the physical things when the spirit departs from them. But when you have the spirit of a thing, you will also have the physical aspect of it. I tell you that possessing the spirituality of something, especially a blessing, is better than the physical of it. If you are spiritually enriched with a blessing, physical blessings will find you and, better said, will walk into your life in no distant time.

Whether the blessing was received by native means or in a Godly way, there are requirements to maintain such blessings. God told the children of Israel in Deuteronomy 28:2, "These blessings shall follow you if…" The "if" aspect is a condition attached to the blessings. In other words, when a new generation is born who suddenly decides they are not interested in fulfilling the conditions attached to the blessings, they lose them.

Some people, born into blessings, do not appreciate the benefits of the conditions attached to their spirituality. Because they have always experienced blessings, they do not know the value of living outside the blessing until they break the covenantal conditions of the blessings.

Jesus said, " Seek first the kingdom of God, and his righteousness, and all other (physical things) will be added to you. It is in the seeking that you get the spirit of a blessing. The kingdom of God is the person of Jesus, so the next word that followed that statement is personified "and his righteousness." You need to pay attention to locating and inheriting the kingdom of God. It is a spiritual place, and you will receive a Spirit that will attract all other things, Mathew 6:33. The seeking is what takes time to do, but once you have found it, everything else will find you.

Conclusion

The Different Forms of God
His Appearances

Moses encountered God differently because of the need for the mission and the purpose of God for the people of Israel. Starting from the burning bush experience, God manifested to Moses in different forms and facets.

Moses' decision to lead the sheep of his father in-law a Midian priest towards the Mount of God was significant to his encounter. This seemingly ordinary decision was profound, hinting at the significance of the encounter about to unfold. This is the same place where God promised Abraham that he would rescue his generation from Egypt after four hundred years. The anticipation of this encounter adds to the intrigue and significance of the narrative.

Moses encountered the God of the Mount, the same Mount on which his forefather Abraham received a promise from the LORD that his people would be rescued from the hands of Pharaoh.

Why am I telling you this? I want you to note the significance of Moses's encounter at the burning bush.

Mount Horeb, also known as the Mount of the LORD, holds significant experiential and historical importance. It was a place of worship and encounter for Abraham, Moses's forefather. His encounter on this Mountain, often referred to as the burning bush encounter was not a mere coincidence but a meticulously predestined event, a pivotal part of a grand divine plan.

In Exodus 3:2 the angel of the LORD who most times is the significance of Jesus appeared to Moses, but the significance of the appearance was not only for Moses to see this angel who later manifested different forms of God to Moses, his eyes were only opened to the things God wanted him to see.

When Moses saw the appearance of the angel of the LORD, other divine beings were present on that Mountain. As I mentioned earlier, this Mountain is a Mountain of many encounters. For Moses to enter this place at this precise moment in his life was a highly strategic setup, a clear indication that it was time for the Israelites to be rescued from Egypt.

When Moses said, I will now turn aside to see this great sight...Exodus 3:3-5, the LORD saw him, and God called him out. A very intriguing moment which was gradually unfolding. Moses encounter here was a representative of the persons of God. The one who initiated the encounter was Jesus, because he is known as the angel of the LORD. The next form of God Moses experienced here was the Holy Spirit who is mostly the representative of God's visuality. God called Moses out of the midst of the bush, Exodus 3:4

What I am saying is this, if you examine the sequence of events from when the angel appeared to Moses until God spoke to him, you can identify three distinct forms of God that Moses encountered. The first was the angel of the LORD (Exodus 3:2), who is believed to be Jesus. The second was the LORD, who represents the Holy Spirit, and God the Father, who started the conversation. This sequence of encounters demonstrates the multifaceted nature of God's physical manifestations.

God said to Moses, "Now you shall see what I will do to Pharaoh; for with a strong hand, he will send them out, and with a strong hand he will drive them out of his land." What God was saying here is, the Pharaoh on the throne differ from the past pharaohs who knew and favored Joseph; the Pharaoh Moses grew up knowing was spearheaded and influenced to destroy the people of God. He told Moses that this Pharaoh would need a form of God that had not been known by any king: a strong hand. This Pharaoh needs a form of God that represents fierce judgment; that's the language this Pharaoh would understand.

To reinforce what God was saying to Moses, for more clarity, God said, "I appeared unto Abraham, unto Isaac, and unto Jacob by the name God Almighty, but I was not known to them by the name Jehovah," Exodus 6:3. Do you understand this statement? God said to Moses, Abraham, Isaac, and Jacob, knew me as God Almighty, but not as Jehovah.

Do you know why? As the LORD stated in Exodus 6:1, Pharaoh would need a different version of God that no one had experienced yet; that version of God is called Jehovah.

What God is also saying here is, Abraham, Isaac, and Jacob didn't need the manifestation of God called Jehovah, they didn't experience bondage; they didn't need God to manifest in any other form than the multi-breasted God, El-Shaddai, the LORD God Almighty.

But today, based on your need and the needs of the people of Israel in Egypt, a different version of me; a different aspect of me, a form of me known as Jehovah will manifest in Egypt.

Abraham, Isaac, and Jacob didn't need the strong hand of the LORD to manifest to them or for them; they were ok, though they encountered hitches here and there, but they were ok; God Almighty was enough for them.

But this generation, according to God Almighty, will need a different version of God because the enemy's wickedness has increased, and the people will not be freed unless there is a distinct manifestation of God that is different from what man is used to.

I feel God arising in this generation, and I feel that the manifestations of the different forms of God are about to hit the earth in a very raw state; this is necessary for man to be reintroduced to God's divinity. The man God created can relate with God better, more like a created being and a god on earth. The church and the world are about to experience a different phase of God, a different shade that is abnormally impossible to man's comprehension.

Therefore, it is very important for man to prepare for this arrival. The physical presence of God is about to shake the earth. When you see the mountains falling into pieces, the mountains smoking up, and fire burning in different places, find out because it may be the physical presence of God that nature is responding to, not a natural disaster.

JESUS in a Different FORM

When Jesus was raised from death by the Holy Ghost, he walked the earth manifesting to his disciples differently. The Bible said in John 20:13-15, when Mary Magdalene was at the tomb of Jesus to check on him but found the tomb empty with the stone taken away. She ran back to alert the disciples, who came and confirmed that it was the truth. Everyone returned to their houses after they confirmed that the body was not in the tomb, but Mary stood there weeping.

When Jesus appeared before her, the Bible says she saw him, but did not recognize him; she thought he was a gardener.

First, how would she think of him as a gardener, out of all people? What form did Jesus appear to Mary that made her feel this way? Was he in grave clothes, or had something else happened to Jesus? Do you remember Jesus went to hell, where he fought battles with the devil, death, and demons and triumphed over them? And he took the keys and was on his way to heaven to present himself to the Father when the tears and the deep groanings of Mary brought him back to the tomb. You would ask how do you know that? He said it right there in the Scripture: "Woman, why do you weep, and whom do you seek?" John 20:15. It would be correct to say that Mary's weeping and seeking drew Jesus back to the grave, the deep groaning of a woman with a passionate love for Jesus. This I say to tell you that when you seek God genuinely, you will encounter and find him. (Mathew 7:7-8).

Mary saw Jesus in a different form, and she could not recognize him but took him to be a gardener. Did he appear as a Gardner because he had just wrought hell in shambles? Is it possible that he looked like someone returning from an intense battle and had the keys in his hand? Was that the reason why Mary thought he was a Gardner? Did Mary Magdalene see Jesus in a raw state, a man with spoils of war heading to the coronation? Jesus told Mary, don't touch me because I have not ascended to my Father.

Let me tell you what happened here: Jesus descended to hell, fought the well-anticipated battle, conquered death, the devil, and all his allies in hell. He sustained some bruises here and there because that's what Genesis 3:15 said: that the seed of the woman will bruise the head of the serpent, and the serpent will bruise his heel. That's exactly what happened in hell that day. Jesus crushed the serpent's head, but he wasn't left without wounds. The serpent also bruised his heels. Therefore, it is written, "he was wounded for our transgression; he was bruised for our iniquities..." Isaiah 53:5.

Mary didn't make a mistake when the Bible said she thought him to be a Gardner; he did look like one, with bruises and some messed-up clothing.

Another episode of Jesus appearing to his disciples in a different form was in John 21:4-7. The Bible recorded that while they were fishing, Jesus appeared to them, but they did not recognize him until Jesus performed a miracle, the same one he performed before he called Peter to service. Again, I ask, why were they unable to recognize Jesus? Was he in a different form?

In another place in the Bible, in Luke 24:15-16, Jesus joins another group of disciples who were on their way to Emmaus; they were unable to recognize him either.

With all the repetitions, I want to conclude this book by saying: this is the time when the LORD is physically walking the earth like he walked the streets in the Garden of Eden. And it is time for man to experience "the only true God" as Jesus faithfully prayed in John 17:3.

That prayer has been answered, and as many as are ready will know God. The true knowledge of God is man's ability to encounter God in a glorious state.

The earth is about to experience God in different forms, but you need to be prepared to see him. Are you ready to experience God in different forms? The manifestations of He that fills all things is here!

Shalom!